Holy PILLOW TALK

Prayers for Intimacy with Jesus
Based on the Song of Songs

AMANDA HILL

COPYRIGHT INFO

2021 Amanda Hill.

All Right Reserved.

Published by Hill House Enterprises, LLC.

www.AmandaHill.org

All right reserved. No part of this publication may be reproduced, stored in a retrieval system, or transmitted in any form, by any means – for example, electronic, mechanical, photocopy, recording, or any other form – without the prior permission of the publisher and author.

Printed in the USA.

First Printing.

Various scripture translations have been used.

New King James Version, NKJV. Copyright 1982 by Thomas Nelson. Used by permission. All rights reserved.

New International Version, NIV Copyright 1973, 1978, 1984, 2011 by Biblica, Inc. Used by permission. All rights reserved worldwide.

New Living Translation, NLT copyright 1996, 2004, 2007, 2013 by Tyndale House Foundation. Used by permission of Tyndale House Publishers Inc., Carol Stream, Illinois 60188. All rights reserved.

The Passion Translation, TPT. Copyright 2017, 2018 by Passion & Fire Ministries, Inc. Used by permission. All rights reserved. ThePassionTranslation.com

Amplified Bible, AMP. Copyright 2015 by The Lockman Foundation. Used by permission. www.lockman.org

King James Version, KJV. Public Domain.

THE MESSAGE, MSG. Copyright 1993, 2002, 2018 by Eugene H. Peterson. Used by permission of NavPress Publishing Group. All rights reserved. Represented by Tyndale House Publisher, Inc.

The Voice, VOICE. Copyright 2012 by Ecclesia Bible Society. Used by permission. All rights reserved.

ISBN: 978-1-7368190-0-5

HOLY PILLOW TALK

DEDICATION

Jesus, this is all for You.

Acknowledgements & Special Thanks

First, unending thanks goes to my amazing family, David, Mason, and Eliana. Without your prodding and patience, I could not have done this. You are my first ministry, my greatest joys, my most favorites, my people. Thank you for loving me.

Thanks to Dad, Mom, and Stacia for all the many years of labor and love to me, as well as the seen and unseen service to the Body of Christ. I am grateful for y'all.

Special thanks to Alison, aka Pumpkin. I sure do love you. Thank you for believing in me.

Huge gratitude to all the pre-readers/pre-editors, loving friends, and special sisters who have faithfully prayed, contended, and warred for and with me. Nothing can be birthed on time without experienced midwives. You know who you are. Thank you. I love you.

Thank you, Melissa for the pictures. You are supernaturally gifted! www.melissaoakleyphotography.com

Diane, you are a patient woman. Thank you for putting up with me and not editing my heart. You have helped me in ways I cannot possibly express. Thank you.

I believe Kingdom people need Kingdom people. I am appreciative for those whom Papa has brought into my life to shape my heart and ministry, to undergird and correct me, to love and push me forward. You are precious and priceless!

Finally, after all these years, I can truly say I am appreciative for the painful betrayals, deep cuts, fierce rejection, harsh and even slanderous words. Critics keep you humble. Enemies make you strong. I am thankful for you.

CONTENTS

Foreword by David Hill
Preface
Introduction

CHAPTER 1: PASSIONATE LOVE | 17
CHAPTER 2: INVITING LOVE | 37
CHAPTER 3: HEALING LOVE | 55
CHAPTER 4: FRUITFUL LOVE | 75
CHAPTER 5: LUKEWARM LOVE | 97
CHAPTER 6: UNTAMED LOVE | 117
CHAPTER 7: COVENANT LOVE | 135

Foreword

It was Monday, May 19, 1997, and I was a senior pastor of a church in our hometown of Givhans, just outside Charleston, SC. I had just finished playing a round of golf when I stopped by the local Christian bookstore, picked up a new cassette tape I had been wanting, and walked to the register. A few moments into the transaction, the pretty salesperson looked up. Seeming to recognize me, she asked if I was David Hill. She knew me, but it took me a moment to assemble the memories. We had met casually about eight years earlier.

The following Monday, Memorial Day of 1997, we went horseback riding on my family's farm---our first date. Months later on Christmas Eve, in the very house we live in today, I asked her to be my wife. Eight months later, in August 1998, Amanda Barrow became Amanda Hill. She was my personal, perfect whirlwind.

As I write this foreword, Amanda and I are only one month from celebrating twenty-two years of marriage. I have witnessed with awe her development as a woman of God. The Lord has used her prophetic voice to guide ministries, businesses, governments, and entertainers. I have watched her pour what the Lord has given her into people in all walks of life, from the least to the greatest. I know her well.

The Lord has given her something to pour into you, too—so pay close attention.

What you are about to read may sometimes become uncomfortable or awkward for you. It did for me. Scripture often refers to the Body of Christ as the "Bride," and to Jesus as the "Bridegroom." The Song of Songs gives us the most refreshing truths about this marriage. Two lovers courting one another, each longing for affection while expressing their own deep love for the other. They come together in marriage, the groom praising the beauty of his new bride as they near the consummation of their union. Even when the bride struggles with her fear of becoming separated from her groom, he reassures her of his affection. What a beautiful picture of Christ and His Church!

Men, when you think of the word "intimacy," what comes to mind? Ask the Lord to reset your assumptions and to teach you His intimacy afresh as you read. Lay down old mindsets and repent of perverted thoughts. He longs for a deep relationship with you. Remember, marriage in the natural reveals what takes place in the spiritual between Jesus and His Bride.

A relationship with Jesus that lacks intimacy produces religion and a performance mentality. But an intimate relationship with Jesus yields presence, power, and provision.

- David Hill

PREFACE

I have never imagined myself an author. I never had the remotest desire to even write a book, so you might understand my consternation and quite honestly, my reluctance, when Holy Spirit presented the idea of this book to me. I suppose that is why this book has taken me nearly two years to complete.

I received the following vision very early in the morning of January 10, 2018, and this book was birthed in that moment. For now, please read the vision and interpretation as follows; I promise to explain more fully in the introduction.

> *I was attending a very well-known Apostolic and Prophetic Center on the East Coast. We were in worship. Suddenly, Jesus appeared, lying on His bed. It was large and opulent, framed by dark, ornately carved wood. The luxurious bedding was adorned in beautiful shades and patterns of blue.*
>
> *I realized Jesus had literally brought His bedroom chamber into the service. Immediately, the atmosphere of the room became extremely awkward. I began to hear the thoughts of the people in the service. "What is He doing here?" "This is unholy and perverted." "This can't be Jesus. Jesus wouldn't do this." "This cannot be worship." "Disgusting."*

He began to silently woo people to come lay down beside Him. Many became even more uneasy and were obviously troubled by His open desire for them. To them, He was ruining their worship service.

When I first saw the bed, I was surprised and somewhat confused. My shock faded as I heard His voice and felt His love. I realized He simply wanted me to let my guard down, to experience His Presence in a deeper, more intimate way.

I pushed through the thoughts of the congregation, as well as my own inhibitions, to lay down beside Jesus on the bed. Resting my head on the pillow next to His, I gazed into His eyes and had a deep, personal encounter with Him. While some people remained stranded in their discomfort and said "No" to His invitation, many others were completely undone, becoming wrecked by gazing into His eyes as they said, "Yes!"

-End of Vision

In November 2017, I was with a friend on a prayer assignment. As we walked, we stumbled upon a French Huguenot settlement. The Huguenots, known as devout believers, built their communities around their places of worship. During the American Revolutionary War, the thirteen colonies were divided between the Patriots (those who fought for freedom from tyranny) and the loyalists (those who were loyal to the crown and wanted to be under the control of the establishment--Great Britain). The Huguenots chose freedom and provided the Patriots with supplies, including wine. Many Huguenots fought on alongside the Patriots during the war.

As we were driving back that evening, I began to weep under the Presence of Jesus, prophesying that a new revolution was coming—but this time, to the Body of Christ. At that moment, I didn't understand what that meant or would look like, but it was clear He was posing a question, and our answer would be either yes or no. Two months later, in January of 2018, I encountered the startling vision of Jesus ushering His bedchamber into that worship gathering.

The setting of that vision was a well-established apostolic center, known for equipping, prophetic training, signs and wonders, flowing in the gifts of Holy Spirit, and the function of the five-fold offices. This apostolic center represents the current apostolic and prophetic movements.

Our spiritual health is directly related to our intimacy with Jesus, and there is no substitute or formula for developing that deep connection with Him. Such deep, genuine connection with the Person of God, our lover Jesus can only be modeled, encouraged, and discovered. He is the source from whom all gifts flow. We need massive reformation in the Body of Christ concerning this epidemic void.

I believe the time has come to shift toward empowered, personal intimacy. We must intentionally practice and teach what intimacy with Jesus looks and sounds like. Because we have had a long famine of intimacy, some have become comfortable, even content, with prostituting His gifts. Worse, some have even attempted to renovate His bedroom chamber into a brothel.

For years, we have ignored the precious invitation back to His holy bedroom because we feel awkward, uncomfortable, and even foreign. In His mercy, He is bringing the bedroom chamber to the Church, where His beckoning can no longer be disregarded.

His invitation is powerful, tender and unmistakable: "Will you come, lay down beside Me, and gaze into My eyes?" This is the question that resounded in me during my encounter of His presence after the Huguenot visit.

The answer to this invitation is either yes or no. To answer yes is the spark of revolution.

To receive His presence and this question with neglect or lukewarm interest will no longer be tolerated. A dividing line is being drawn. He is challenging us to transform from performing like the Body to simply being His ravished Bride. Holiness, passion, the fear of the Lord and intimacy are returning to the Bride of Christ.

Those who answer a wholehearted yes are the patriots, the pioneers who will arise for the new reformation. This will affect every sphere of influence and every mountain of culture. These brave patriots desire freedom. Giving themselves to intimacy with Jesus ensures them eternal spiritual liberty.

Regrettably, some will say no. These are the loyalists, devoted to the establishment and led by a controlling, religious spirit. Their reply sounds like, "What is He doing here?" "This is unholy and perverted." "This can't be Jesus. Jesus wouldn't do this." "This is abnormal and cannot be worship." "Disgusting." They misunderstand intimacy with Jesus, categorizing it as excessive, flaky, and laborious.

For decades, we have cried out for the awakening of the nations of the earth. We have heard it prophesied that revival is coming, that we are on the brink of the greatest harvest of souls ever seen. Who doesn't want to see a billion-soul harvest for our Father's Kingdom?

I believe the harvest we will see—in our own lives, families, ministries, cities, regions, states, nations, and mountains of influence—will be directly proportional to our intimacy with Jesus. In the natural, we know that physical intimacy must take place before a baby can be birthed. The spiritual realm mirrors the natural realm in perpetuity. Intimacy is the catalyst for authentic signs, wonders, and miracles, all of which will contribute to bringing forth the greatest harvest we have ever seen.

There will be pockets of believers who arise to pioneer and steward this revolution. This devoted service will come with great persecution from those who are loyalists of the religious establishment. Yet it will come with even greater reward from our Bridegroom. Do not be deceived; this revolution will come with great cost. There will be relationships lost and friendships broken due to your yes to lay down with Jesus.

As your religious mountains are brought low and new pathways form within you, allow others to experience your transformation—for indeed, you will be changed. Model intimacy with dauntless trust, even when you feel conspicuous. When we lie beside Him under the blue bedding of communion, fresh revelation flows.

INTRODUCTION

Sometimes prophets communicate in a scattered manner. It is a daunting challenge to assemble the heavenly words in our spirits, and it takes practice to serve them to the Body of Christ in a palatable way that is easy to receive and digest. For many years, my prophetic experiences consisted of meaningful numbers, license plates, expressions of nature, dreams, and visions. However, the Lord eventually ceased from speaking to me in those well-travelled ways, and I thought He had gone silent. That was incorrect. He was teaching me other ways He wanted to communicate with me! As a result, I am learning to remain present and attentive at every moment, because He is constantly communicating with us! It is important for us to recognize His voice in every form.

In October 2018, my husband David and I were blessed to go to Israel. Before our trip, the Lord began highlighting the numbers 318 (three eighteen), and throughout our trip, we were repeatedly inundated with sightings of 3-18. Upon arriving back to the States, David happened to look at the license plate on his new truck. Can you guess what it read? XXX-318.

Our curiosity piqued, we began researching the Hebraic significance of the numbers 3-18. (Important note: Each Hebrew letter has a corresponding numerical value.) We found that the sum of these numbers calculated to be the name *Eliezar*.

Our spirits leapt when we read the story from Genesis 24. For the sake of space and time, we will simplify what we found, but we searched and studied in depth and were profoundly changed by the word of the Lord we discovered!

Eliezar was Abraham's chief servant, a position of substantial authority. He was entrusted by Abraham to leave their household in Canaan, "the land of promise," to find a wife for Isaac from among Abraham's relatives. At this time, Abraham was advanced in age and Sarah had recently died.

Eliezar journeyed to Haran (present day Turkey). Abraham's relatives had settled in Haran after leaving Ur of the Chaldeans in Mesopotamia (present day Iraq). The journey from Canaan to Haran was long and dangerous, so Eliezar's expedition would have taken a minimum of three to four weeks.

Eliezar arrived at a well just outside the city with a caravan of ten camels, loaded with numerous expensive gifts. He asked for God to give him a sign to indicate the virgin who was destined to be Isaac's bride. Graciously, the Lord answered his request when Rebekah not only offered Eliezar a drink, but also volunteered to water his caravan of camels!

Eliezar discovered Rebekah was from Abraham's family line. Per Eliezar's request, and the customs of hospitality of that time, Rebekah extended an invitation for him to stay with her family. Prior to the meal, Eliezar plainly shared his mission to find Isaac a bride. Everyone in the family, from her brother to her parents, agreed that Rebekah should return with Eliezar to Canaan. They recognized the direction and will of the Lord regarding this proposed marriage.

However, when it was time for them to leave the next morning, Rebekah's brother, Laban, and mother, Milcah, suggested the trip be delayed by ten days. Eliezar received this opinion reluctantly; he was eager to return to Isaac with the bride he was longing for. All eyes fell to Rebekah, who would be the tie breaker. When asked if she was willing to go with Eliezar immediately, her answer was, "yes."

With her farewell calls of her family fading to the horizon behind her, Rebekah and her childhood nurse, Deborah, travelled with the caravan on the long journey to Canaan. Soon, Isaac and Rebekah met face-to-face, and she became his wife.

The imagery of this story deeply intrigues me. Rebekah had never seen Isaac. She was leaving her homeland, her family, and everything she knew to join in covenant with a man—a stranger—who was hundreds of miles away. As I studied, I sensed in my spirit there must have been something that compelled her to leave her place of comfort, even after the opportunity to delay her departure.

During the Genesis account of this story, Isaac was around forty years old, and Eliezar was eighty-five. Eliezar had served Abraham for over sixty years. He would have had a front-row seat to the whole story of Isaac's life, including Sarah's extended infertility, the unexpected promise of Isaac's conception, the wait for God's promise to be fulfilled, Sarah's geriatric pregnancy and birth, Isaac's eventful childhood, and now, his full maturity as Abraham's promised heir, yet without a wife.

Eliezar, in carrying his master's heart, would have been unquestionably invested in Abraham and Isaac's happiness.

I wholeheartedly believe that Eliezar, who knew Isaac as well as his parents, spoke so highly of him that Rebekah was eager to meet her anticipated bridegroom. Eliezar represented his master Isaac well, with unimpeachable integrity and loyalty. He was the perfect delegate to speak on Isaac's behalf. I can only imagine the conviction and affection of his beautiful words describing Isaac, such that Rebekah was wholly persuaded to leave at once.

As David and I took hold of all that Holy Spirit was revealing to us, we longed for confirmation. In November 2018, I attended a prophet's roundtable meeting in Florida. One of the guest speakers—ironically, the leader of the very church I had seen in my vision—caught my full attention. I listened for what seemed like ten minutes, soaking up every word, but when I checked the recording on my phone, the audio was two and a half hours! His next words perfectly summarized what David and I had been seeing, sensing, studying, and praying over for months:

"I do think the Lord gave me what is going to be the most important anointing, or what is now the most important anointing we can have. The Lord said it was the Eliezar anointing. Just think about what he did. He never talked about himself. It was always about his master. Somehow, he caused Rebekah to fall so in love with Isaac that she was willing to leave everything and go. What kind of an anointing is that?

"I think the greatest anointing we could have is that which would compel the Bride to love the Bridegroom, that she would love Him so much that she would just be willing to leave everything to pursue Him. That anointing is coming. I think we have a measure of it, but I think it's going to grow, so when the Bride says, "Come," He comes."

As I relistened to his words that evening, I was a weeping, snotty, shaking wreck. All of the pieces of this revelation from the Lord, in more detail than we have time to explore here, profoundly shook me. The vision of the bed in that worship gathering, the revelation of Eliezar's beautiful spirit, and my experience in that prophetic gathering fell together seamlessly. Holy Spirit arranged every piece to this very delicate and intricate puzzle.

In the months and years since this mantle was first laid upon us, David and I have felt the weight of our calling, in this anointing to draw the Bride of Jesus back to Him. As the Body of Christ enters this new era of intimacy, I hope this book lends a piece of the answer to nurturing deeper intimacy with Jesus.

The words of this book are meant to be prayed and decreed out loud. Romans 10:17 says, "So faith comes from hearing [what is told], and what is heard comes by the [preaching of the] message concerning Christ." I believe when we open our mouth to proclaim what Jesus says and how He feels about us, we are preaching faith to ourselves. As a result, our spirit man increases, heals, and matures!

As we speak aloud, we not only increase our faith in agreement with His perfect will, but we also forbid the enemy from attacking these areas. Jesus is the Word, and nothing is more powerful than Him.

In Hebrew, Rebekah's name means, "captivating." My deepest cry is that as you read these prayers and decrees aloud, you will shake off the awkwardness and inhibitions that currently weaken your ideas of intimacy. I pray we, the Bride of Christ, become captivated with our Bridegroom, Jesus, the Lover of our soul—like Rebekah did Isaac.

How to Read This Book

For nearly 20 years, I have taken scriptures, prophetic words, sermons, dreams, and visions and turned them into personal prayers—conversations between Jesus and me. I wholeheartedly believe as we audibly decree the *rhema* (the spoken word of God) mixed with the *logos* (the written word of God), we are more effective in every facet of our discipleship and relationship with Jesus.

What you are about to read are prayers and decrees from the Song of Songs, laced with my own personal prayers and decrees from my journals. I have used several different versions of scripture to capture the passion of the heart of Jesus for His church. Please take note of when the Bride (you) is speaking to Jesus, her Bridegroom, and when He is speaking to you, the Bride.

This book is meant to be read aloud, as a dialogue between lovers. Each chapter fits easily into fifteen minutes, perhaps as an ideal component of your daily devotion time with the Lord. However, you might also choose to go more slowly, deliberately surrendering to an all-encompassing, extended journey of intimacy with Jesus.

Some of the language may feel uncomfortable to speak; you may even find it risqué. Please consider that there is a reason Solomon wrote his Song of Songs, and why it is included in the Bible. Many have debated this book's symbolism and true meaning. Personally, I believe it was written so we can give our Bridegroom, Jesus, the worshipful intimacy He truly desires. What if we have missed out on His deeper realms of glory due to our inability to speak out and walk in the intimacy of true, complete devotion with Him?

My hope is to walk in the anointing of Eliezar, initiating the Bride to fall in love with her Bridegroom through this passionate journey. I pray that this book will be the beginning of a deeper love affair between you and Jesus. May there be no wall, no boundaries, and no veil in your love story.

Prior to each chapter is a brief overview titled, "What You Might Experience". This concise introduction is specifically created to prepare your heart for what the chapter is intended to accomplish. The dialogue between you, the Bride, and Jesus, your Bridegroom, can invoke a deluge of emotions. Following this paragraph, some thoughts from other readers are included, entitled "What Others Experienced." These testimonies will offer further insight into what you might anticipate as you read.

At the end of each chapter appears a section entitled, "Deeper Still." These thoughtful questions will help you in your journey towards greater intimacy and are designed to assist you in processing any uncomfortable dialogue you read within the chapters. Two pages of blank space are included as well; use them to write your own love notes to Jesus. I strongly encourage you to take advantage of both sections, as they are fashioned to expand your passion and deepen your intimacy with Him.

Shallow intimacy results in weak authority. I believe the Song of Songs is the most important book in the Bible. By describing how our intimacy with Jesus can be fostered and forged, it lays the foundation for authentic, love-driven authority to blossom.

Jesus is the most priceless gift given, for without Him the Song of Songs has no meaning. He is the entire context for understanding and fulfilling the invitations of this book. I have personally fallen in love with this beautiful love story. In the process of writing this book, my own passion with Jesus deepened. Truly, I cannot wait for you to experience Him in this new way!

I invite you to pray the following prayer, fully diving into your divine destiny as an intimate lover of Jesus—your Bridegroom!

PRAYER

Jesus, I admit I have not fully, intimately given myself to You---at least not in the way You have longed for. Forgive me for my ignorance. Forgive me for my selfishness. I want to love You the way You want to be loved, not just in the way that suits me. As I bravely engage in our conversations through this book, melt away my awkwardness and any preconceived opinions. Free me from what is comfortable and convenient. Let me fully give You what You really desire: *me.*

So, here I am, arms and heart wide open. I am ready to enter into our "Holy Pillow Talk".

In the entire world there is nothing to equal the day on which the Song of Songs was given to Israel."

— Akiba ben Joseph, Jewish rabbi

Chapter 1
PASSIONATE LOVE

What You Might Experience...

Chapter One is filled with romantic language and descriptive poetry. There may be an occasion or two where you want to stop reading aloud, due to your own inhibitions and embarrassment. Do your best to push through these moments of hesitation. As you move forward, you will experience His Presence in a way you never have before. It will be worth any temporary apprehension you may encounter.

What Others Experienced...

"This chapter opens with full discomfort. I have never ever considered intimacy with Jesus like this. However, once I continued to read aloud, I began to experience a new level of awareness of Him like I've never felt before. The feeling of His Presence lasted not only while reading, but also continued throughout the day. It made my prayers deeper, more relational, and closer. I was far more aware of Him all day long, more aware than I ever have been."

"I have always considered my relationship with Jesus to be close, so I couldn't imagine I would be uncomfortable with the concept of intimacy. However, the opening line struck me as risqué. I was confronted with the truth that I have become comfortable viewing Him as Father but have not allowed Him to love me as a Bridegroom, as a Husband."

"This chapter reminded me I needed to talk more affectionately, and more often, with Jesus. I also realized my conversations with Him lately haven't been as tender and passionate as I want them to be."

REMEMBER:
SPEAK THESE WORDS ALOUD.

The Bride speaks:

Jesus, I want You. Just You.

I want to know what Your lips are like. Come and overwhelm me with Your savory kisses over and over again.

I taste and see how good You are.

I want to know what Your touch feels like. Embrace me, and it will intoxicate me more than the sweetest vintage wine.

I drink You in.

I want to know what You smell like.
Release the aroma of Your extraordinary fragrance.

I breathe You in.

I want to know what Your voice sounds like.
Say my name and I am undone.

I listen intently to every word You speak.

I want to know what You look like.
Let me see You. I want nothing more than to behold the beauty of Your handsome face.

Hear and answer my desire for You.

I wait in expectation.

Your lovely name is like precious, scented oil, poured out. It is no wonder You are adored.

Draw me into Your heart. Take me away with You. Take me away from the noise, from everything that rivals my affection for You. Let us run away together. Let us enter Your chamber, the Holy of Holies.

We will rejoice with singing and dancing there, for You have awakened the longing within me.

I have said before, "I want to know what love is."

Now I see: Love is a Person.

Love is You. You are Love.

In this moment, I have one desire: show me Yourself. Show me Who You are and what You are like.

I want to know everything about You.
I want to know everything about love.
You are perfect love.

Come and baptize me in Your perfect love and drown every ounce of fear. Flood me completely until all timidity and anxiety surrender to Your sovereignty.

My heart is broken and worn out.
I am weary and in desperate need.

I lost focus while tending to the vineyards of others and have become bone dry. My soul is parched, like a wasteland desert. I attempted to please the religious crowd, but those vines are reluctant to bear fruit. I am burned out from constant work and performance. I believed I could earn my freedom and position with You.

Jesus, I am so tired. I have enough energy only to fall into Your refreshing embrace.

Your name is Rest, and I am stealing away with You.

With You, I recover my life and find still waters.

With You, I experience peace that surpasses my understanding. This peace guards my heart and mind.

I put my ear to Your chest and listen to Your steady heartbeat, learning the melodious rhythms of Your grace and mercy.

You are entirely humble and gentle, and Your even pulse resets the chaotic rattle in my chest.

With You, there is no religious confinement, no legalistic restraints, no institutional bondage. There is only our loyal covenant relationship. With You, there is no heavy burden to bear.

Rescue me from my constricting religious box. It has restrained me from loving You, from fully giving myself to You. Jesus, would You completely destroy this box so that I cannot return to it?

I take off my filthy rags of self-righteousness, overjoyed to trade them for Your royal robes of righteousness. I notice I am beginning to smell like You as Your garments rub on my skin.

I decree: Today is a new day.

I abandon my bonds, the dry fields of slavery to man's opinions and religious traditions. I choose to cultivate this vineyard of our relationship.

You have been waiting here for me, so here I am.

This is You and me, together.

When I look into Your face, I am transformed into Your image. My full affection is Yours.

You have my undivided attention.

Every worry fades when I look into Your eyes. The darkness in me becomes light. You embrace my darkness, shattering it wide open with Your perfect love and light.

The haunting cages of control and confinement are finally being crushed. I am becoming free!

I do not have to perform or compete to gain Your attention. I do not have to labor to win Your affection. I cannot earn You, for You have given all of Yourself to me. You are my home, my safe place, my hiding place, my secret place.

I do not have to strive to be seen or heard by You, because You are always listening to me.
With You I am heard.

I do not have to shout to make You look my way, because You are already watching me. With You, I am known and seen.

I do not have to prove my worthiness. With You, I am worthy and have all I need.

You cherish me and call me priceless. I belong to You.

Change my paradigm. Teach me to receive and not achieve.

This truth frees me from insecurity that drives me to competition and performance. What a gift this is! What a gift You are!

Tell me what You want to do today, my Love.

HOLY PILLOW TALK

Where are You working? Let us partner together. Lead me, for I am Your Beloved.

I just want to be where You are, do what You do, see what You see, and say what You say. I want to love what You love and hate what You hate. I do not want to miss a thing. I tear down any veil or barrier that stands between us.

Let me feel what You feel, be wrapped around You, and summed up in You.

Your Presence cures my loneliness. It heals my brokenness. It breaks my sadness and depression.

I have unspeakable joy when I am with You.

All my discouragement and hopelessness are washed away, for Your joy is contagious. It strengthens me. Despair and darkness flee from me.

When I am with You, I laugh and smile.
When I am with You, I feel free.
When I am with you, I release my need to control.

So come and do whatever You want to.

When I am with You, I am alive.

Jesus, my Bridegroom, responds:

My Beauty, when I created you, it was love at first sight.

You are stunningly radiant and lovely! I long for you to grasp My amazing love for you. I do not want you to doubt it for a moment.

Come. Be rooted and established in My love.

Let Me help you hold to the truth:
My love for you is wider than the widest valley,
longer than the longest river,
higher than the highest mountain,
and deeper than the deepest ocean.

When I look at you, I see My friend. I see My treasure.
You are breathtakingly exquisite to Me.

Your eyes are stunning, passionate, and gentle. Like dove's eyes, you have one single focus. You only have eyes for Me, and I only have eyes for you.

Be diligent. Keep your eyes fixed on Me.

Find comfort in knowing you positively thrill Me.

When I gaze upon you, I see your strength. I see your royalty.

You belong here with Me. Do not doubt your position. You are Mine. We speak face to face, and you glow with My authority.

My Father, Holy Spirit and I made you holy and joyfully bright. We prepared for you a string of jewels, gold earrings and beads of silver.

I trust you with My authority, as one refined by My purifying fire. I am removing the debris, dross, wood, hay, and stubble, until all that remains is gold, silver, and costly stones.

You have been marked, set apart, and chosen.

Come and enjoy the place of shelter and refuge which I have provided for you. I know exactly what you need. You can find fulfillment in Me.
I promise, only I can truly satisfy you.

You are so deeply loved that I offered My own body and blood to redeem you. Your name is carved upon My heart and engraved on My hand. You stand in complete victory because of My sacrifice. My blood bought priceless freedom for you. This is why I Am so jealous for you!

Take a moment to truly take hold of what I did for you.

The nail driven through My feet, severing skin, nerves, and tendons, bought back your dominion and authority. Every power that rises against you is under your feet. Every place your foot touches I have given to you to establish My Kingdom.

Understand this with absolute clarity:
I have imparted to you all My authority to trample over the Kingdom of Darkness. You will crush every demon and overcome every power. Absolutely nothing will be able to harm you as you walk in your rightful dominion. I have eternally established you, and all my church, to express My government on the earth, legislating in the authority and purity of My holy love.

The nails driven through My hands, slicing joints and ligaments, redeemed your ability to succeed, prosper, and receive divine inheritance. My blood-stained palms broke the curse from your hands, freeing you to lift your holy, purified hands in worship.

Beloved, I charge you this day: use your hands to manifest miracles, signs, and wonders, driving out demons in My name. Lay your hands upon the sick and see them healed.

Your hands are blessed. I will make you abundantly prosper in all the works of your hands, for I delight in you.

The crown of thorns the soldiers pressed into the flesh of My skull purchased healing for your mind. You are liberated from mental torment. My wonderful peace now transcends your human understanding and will guard your heart and mind. All bondage, sickness, infirmities, and diseases of your mind are healed. I make you free from every corrupted thought: stress, anxiety, compulsions, confusion, distractions, forgetfulness, mind corruptions, heaviness, weariness, worry, insomnia, fears, and phobias. Mental yokes and oppression slide from you, for I give you My mind and My thoughts.

You have a new mind. You have the authority to capture every faulty thought pattern. Command them to bow in obedience to My powerful name. I Am never weary or tired. I never slumber or sleep. Let Me remind you: I have never lost a battle, and I never will.

Trust Me fully to heal your mind.

Blood and water poured from My side when the spear pierced Me. My utter anguish and bursting chest healed your broken heart and emotions. I restored you to wholeness, never-ending hope and inexpressible joy. I Am faithful to clean and bandage your wounds, and to comfort you in the midst of your hurt. Despair, hopelessness, sadness, depression, discouragement, and all other ungodly emotions are defeated by My sacrifice.

Just as the Spirit of the Lord was upon Me, so it is also upon you! You are anointed to be hope for the poor, freedom for the brokenhearted, and new eyes for the blind. Preach and declare to prisoners, "You are set free!" Let the testimony of My faithfulness to you cause you to raise your voice!

I was severely beaten and bruised. I bled internally and externally. The abuse I endured ripped Me open. Blood flowed from My neck, shoulders, and back. When the crowds saw Me, they were horrified. My face was so disfigured that I hardly looked human. I was despised and rejected---a man of deep sorrows, intimately acquainted with suffering. Everyone was disgusted by Me and turned their backs on Me.

Yet, I bore your weaknesses and grief.

I willingly carried your sorrows and endured the torment of your sufferings. Though they viewed me as a criminal worthy of punishment, I have never sinned. Yet I was pierced for your rebellious deeds and transgressions. I was crushed for your iniquities and sin. I was beaten so you could be completely whole, experiencing peace, prosperity, and wellbeing.

I was whipped so you could be healed. I broke every curse for you. There is no accident, injury, infirmity, disease or sickness I cannot heal. I am greater than all of these; they must bow down to My Name. My body was broken so that yours could be completely whole, healthy, and healed.

I Am more than enough for you. Just believe Me.

The Father laid your sins on Me. My crimson flow redeemed and unshackled you. I was willing to endure it all because I love you. To me, Beloved, you are worthy of My sacrifice.

There is nothing I would not do for you, My Lovely One.

Undone, the Bride worships:

Jesus, You have lived out Your unreserved love for me. How can I possibly thank You for all You have done?

Yes, You are my only atonement. Your sacrifice for me compels me to love You more. The revelation of Your suffering love rests over my heart.

I will never forget what You have done for me.

The pressing, the pain, and the persecution You endured for my freedom drives me to my knees in gratitude. I am released from condemnation, shame and judgment. I admit I will never understand how much it cost You to purchase my freedom. You bore it all just to be with me. It is more than I can comprehend.

You never sinned or deceived anyone. You did not retaliate when You were insulted, and You never threatened revenge. You personally carried my sins in Your body on the cross, so that I can be dead to the darkness of sin and rise to the high standard of Your brilliant life.

Your wounds have healed me.

You redeemed me so I can sit at Your table in constant communion with You. You saved a seat just for me. It has my name on it.

I remember and honor Your sacrifice. Your broken body and spilled blood are my food and drink.

They are my life, and You are my portion.

I abide in You and You abide in me.

May the fragrance of my thankfulness captivate You, Jesus.

I break open all of me, all that I hold valuable. I pour myself out on You as a sign of my fidelity. May the atmosphere be filled with my deep affection and unending praise. I have no doubt I belong with You.

You are handsome! You are charming, far more pleasing than anything I have ever experienced before. Our bridal chamber is anointed, fragrant and fruitful, just like the forest trees after a long, slow, gentle rain.

I pledge to run after You. I will pursue You.

My love for You is not temporary. It is neither fleeting nor fading.

With You is where I want to be. May my passionate love for You be evident and unbridled.

With You is where I belong.

Song of Songs 1, Psalm 34:8, Matthew 11:28, Philippians 4:7, Nehemiah 8:10, I John 4:18, Isaiah 49, Matthew 27, Deuteronomy 30, Mark 16, Isaiah 61, Joshua 1, Luke 4, Psalms 147, Psalms 121, Ephesians 3:17-18, 1 Corinthians 3, Isaiah 52, Matthew 26:6-13, 1 Peter 2, John 6

Deeper Still
Chapter 1, Passionate Love

1. The first few paragraphs are intimately descriptive. Was there any portion that caused you to feel awkward or uncomfortable? If yes, why did you feel that way? Now list the items/words that provoked the awkwardness and ask Holy Spirit to remove these blockages in your heart, mind and emotions.

2. Have you felt confined by religious traditions or the opinions of men? How have these constrictions stifled your intimacy with Jesus?

3. Are there any Christian leaders or churches you need to forgive? Maybe you worked their vineyard and were treated with inferiority. Perhaps you experienced spiritual abuse. Take a few moments and say their names aloud, releasing forgiveness toward them and in turn, healing in you.

4. As you read the portion where Jesus describes His sacrifice for you, what emotions stirred within you? Have you felt you had to strive to attain Jesus' affection or shout to gain His attention? If yes, do you know how or where this ungodly belief crept in? Ask Him about it and listen for His answer. Additionally, reread pages 25-28 and let His words sink deep into your being, washing away any striving, unworthiness, and illegitimacy.

5. Is there a particular portion of this chapter you need to read again, claiming healing for yourself? If so, decree it aloud again, placing your hand on the area(s) that need to experience the healing of Jesus. Write down what you sense, feel, see, smell, taste, and/or hear.

PERSONAL LOVE NOTES TO JESUS

HOLY PILLOW TALK

Personal Love Notes to Jesus

Chapter 2
INVITING LOVE

What You Might Experience . . .

Chapter Two is laced with invitations from Jesus. They may expose the areas of your life you fear His love might not reach. His passion-filled words will help His perspective of you to solidify within you. Allow His expressive, tender tone to transform your own thoughts about yourself.

Remember: what you think turns into words. Your words then shape your behavior, and your behavior determines your life. Let His words penetrate the marrow of your being.

What Others Experienced . . .

> "When I read this chapter, I felt a rekindling for more intimacy with Him. It stirred my emotions and my senses to reconnect in that way."

> "Reading this chapter deepened my understanding of how extensively He loves me. In turn, I'm more confident in our relationship, bringing to Him any and every concern."

> "I felt a release of guilt and shame as I read this chapter. I am finally realizing nothing can separate me from Him, not even my past."

The Bride Speaks:

Jesus, I am Your focus, the very theme of Your song.

You write melodies about our love and sing them over me. Your songs of deliverance surround me and protect me from harm and danger. You take great delight in me, quieting me with Your love and rejoicing over me with singing.

When You sing over me, it takes my breath away. Nothing is more romantic than the sound of Your love song to me. You have captured my heart and filled my eyes with wonder.

You have completely won me over.

Your voice is beyond description.

It's powerful,
yet gentle,
thundering and full of force,
but peaceful.

Your voice sounds like roaring waters and sacred music all at the same time.

Jesus, there are simply are no words to describe Your fragrance, the quaking effect of Your Presence. It is obvious when You walk into the room. *Everything* changes.

It is impossible for any atmosphere to resist the Voice of Life. It is the sound of my very fibers.

You break open hard, dry places, and resurrect them with fruitfulness and purpose. You break into impossible situations and defeated circumstances, overcoming them with hope, life, and abundance. You break through fear, doubt, and unbelief; they are sabotaged by miracles, healing, and restoration.

Breakthrough is not just what You do. It is Who You are.

You are the Breaker! Death bows. Chains shatter. Sickness flees. Darkness scatters. Troubles vanish. Worries fade. Depression ceases. Unbelief caves.

There is no shadow in Your glory. You are incomparable and without equal, mighty and magnificent. I feel eclipsed by awe.

All I want to do is sit here, wrapped in Your reality, under the shadow of Your glory, tasting and savoring Your delicious love. I blossom and rest in Your gaze. Your Presence hovers over me, ensuring I grow deep and strong in You.

You transform the entire landscape of my being, down to the marrow. The hopeless wilderness within me now flourishes with joy. Every dry and barren place bursts forth with abundant blooms, producing new fruit. No detail of my life has gone untended. No one could ever care for me like You do.

When I see Your glory, Your beautiful majesty, I am established and energized. Discouragement and defeat leave me.
Because You are the strength of my life, I lay my fear aside.

When I thought I would perish, Your love for me was stirred up. You raced to my rescue! When my thoughts became chaotic and out of control, You came with Your soothing comfort, calming me down and bringing overwhelming relief.

It is impossible to describe Your invincible peace.

You obliterate every obstacle to give me victory, waving Your banner of love over me. I am protected and adored! Thank You for being my Defender and Savior!

You never have and never will stop fighting for me. You are a Man of War, and Your victory is complete. You cause me to consistently triumph! No one can raise their fist to You. You promise no weapon intended to harm me will succeed, for You are Jehovah Nissi, my Perfect Protector and Promise Keeper. This Is Your name.

Your battle record is perfect. You are undefeatable! You can do anything but fail!

I am lovesick for You, craving what refreshes and sustains. I am longing for more, yet how could I ever endure it? Surely it would be more than I can take!

Yet, though the thought is overwhelming, I still ache for You to pull me even closer and take me deeper still. My head rests in Your left arm while Your right hand pulls me close to You. You whisper how much You adore me, and my ear hums with Your breath. Your words are refreshing and tender.

Nothing can stop You from being near me.

Who could ever separate me from Your endless love? Nothing has the power to diminish Your love towards me. Troubles, pressures, distress, persecutions, danger, and death threats are unable to come between You and me. These threats are toothless when compared to Your almighty love. Because of You, I am triumphant in all things. I am more than a conqueror, empowered by Your grace, which is without rival.

You are Master over everything.

I am convinced that Your love conquers death, hardships, demons, fear about today, and worries about tomorrow. Not even the power of hell can separate me from You. No power in the sky above or in the earth below – indeed, nothing in all creation will ever be able to distance me from You.

Absolutely nothing can stop Your love for me.

You spring with joy over the mountains, leaping in love over the hills that attempt to divide us. You move smoothly and swiftly to come to me.

Yet, even in my eagerness for you, Jesus, I have to admit: I feel apprehension as You move closer to me. I am scared. There are things I have kept from You. I have harbored secret separations in my life. Some of my heart is walled high and thick, I have never let anyone into these dark rooms of pain. They are full of regret, sorrow and unbearable hurt.

To welcome You there is uncharted territory.

Believing You love me enables me to lower my guard. No obstacles can stop Your love for me, but what about my mistakes and failures? What about my past? There are things no one knows, things I cannot talk about.

When You see what I have hidden, will You still want me? It's dark there and I am ashamed.

You unnerve me as You gaze into my sinful soul. I know You want me to let You in, but I feel guilt and embarrassment to let You fully see the real me.

JESUS, MY BRIDEGROOM, RESPONDS TO ME:

You, My Love, are My soulmate.
My Father set you aside just for Me.

When I say nothing can separate Me from you, that is what I mean: *nothing* you have done or will do can scare Me away. Do you think you have gone too far or done too much to make Me love you less?

That is impossible.

Don't let the enemy's voice speak louder than Mine. He has been lying to you. All he does is lie. Do not believe anything he speaks. Stop listening to him.

Now, invite Me in.

When you let Me walk into your dark, painful, hidden places, I fill them with light, healing, and wholeness. Do not be embarrassed or ashamed. I will never give up on you. I do not leave when things get hard.

I Am not like the others who have hurt you.
You can trust Me.

My Father sees you as He sees Me: blameless. Hear me again, those hidden places and secret rooms cannot make Me love you any less.

Now take My hand; we can walk through those places together. Let Me go with you there, and I will release deliverance and inner healing to your body, mind and emotions.

Look into My eyes.

Let Me show you what is to come for us.

I find great delight and pleasure in you. The curse of sin tries to tempt you, but you still remain steadfast and pure in My sight.

Now arise and soar with Me.

Let Me take you to new heights. I promise to take you to places you have never been before. It is time to forget the former things; they are all past you now. I am doing something brand new, something that has never been done or even heard of before. Even now it is sprouting up, growing and maturing faster than you know.

Can you see it? Do you believe it?

Even if the grass withers and the flowers fade, My Word will stand forever. Snow and rain fall from Heaven and water the earth. They do not return to Heaven until they have accomplished their purpose in soaking the earth and causing it to spout with new life, providing seed for the farmer and bread to the hungry.

The words that I speak are just the same. They will not return to Me without results. It is impossible for them to be unfulfilled.

My words always produce fruit. Always. They must perform My purpose. They must prosper and fulfill the assignment I sent them to accomplish.

I Am your Kinsman Redeemer. I Am calling you to come to Me. Let Me show you how much I love you. I will not leave or abandon you. Mountains may move, hills disappear, but My faithful love for you is steadfast. It will remain.

Nothing and no one can shake My covenant of shalom with you.

I Am going to show you My heart. I Am going to tell you My deep secrets. You asked Me to be close to you and here I Am. I Am drawing you into My heart.

Now is the time! The season has changed! The bondage of the unfruitful winter has ended, and the dark clouds and rain have come and gone. Brilliant, spring flowers are blossoming all over. The time for singing has arrived. The momentum of harvest is building. The sounds of cooing doves announce heaven's arrival in your heart. Can you hear their melody? The air is heavy with sounds that awaken you and move you forward.

I Am commanding the weighty fruit of breakthrough harvest to come forth within you now.

Beloved, no eye has seen, no ear has heard, and no mind can imagine what I have prepared for you.

Listen closely. Increase is coming! Overflow is coming! Multiplication is coming!

Now, enlarge your tent and make room for more. Stretch out the curtains of your dwelling and spare no expense! Lengthen your tent ropes and strengthen the tent pegs firmly in the ground. For you will increase exponentially and spread out in every direction. Soon you will be bursting at the seams!

You, your sons, and your daughters will take possession of nations and will revitalize deserted cities. You will conquer and possess enemy gates and nations.

Do not fear. Do not be ashamed. Do not grieve. Do not be oppressed. You are not inadequate. You are enough. I Am the One who commands Heaven's Angel Armies, and they are coming to help you. You are not alone.

Let your faith arise and come into agreement with this shift! Dormancy has ceased. Leave the old and step into the new with Me. Let your paradigm be flexible, for things will not be as they always have been.

Truly, I make all things new. You have not been this way before.

Humility and trust are your greatest assets. So, come now, My Delight, discern clearly and quickly. This new day of awakening and destiny is breaking forth in, around, and through you! My purpose and plans for you are bursting forth! The vines are in blossom and their fragrance whispers, "Change is here."

Therefore, arise and come with Me. We are going to the higher place; the time has come to make your home in My heavenlies. My secret place will become your home, so settle in. Do not be shy and hide yourself from Me. Let Me see your beautiful face and hear your lovely voice. Nothing satisfies Me more than when you speak My name. To Me, your voice is delicious, and your face is radiant.

Leave behind your seclusion and learn to crave My light.

Lovely one, you must catch the little foxes that trouble and hinder our relationship. They are sly as they try to spoil our budding vineyard, our garden of love. Do not let them ruin what I have planted within you. Do not let hidden compromises stop My fruit from growing and flourishing within you.

I will help you. Let Me help you. We will catch and remove them together.

Come now. I am inviting you into My love. You do not have to do anything. Just enter into My rest. When you rest in Me, it creates joy! Set everything else aside. Just be with Me. I want to be closer than your own breath, closer than your own skin. Every obligation and distraction on your list can wait. They are secondary to being with Me. I Am what you need. Your place is with Me.

So, come away with Me, My Beauty. My heart burns to be with you. I Am calling, drawing, and pursuing you. Linger in this place with Me. Do not rush off. Do not hurry away. Set plenty of time aside. You can do it.

We need to be together. Me in you, and you in Me. Trust Me. I know what is best for you. We do not even have to talk. Just lay down here beside Me.

Let Me hold you for a while.

I, His Bride, Respond:

You are mine and I am Yours.

I find everything I need in You.

We fully delight ourselves in one another.

Please dissolve my fear and teach me to make Your courage my portion.

I hunger to go away with You, Jesus. The invitation to experience Your Presence in a new way provokes my desire. Thank You for calling and choosing me!

The craving of my heart is to accept the call to be set apart. I long to ascend to the mountain of consecration and holiness. I feel as though I have been awaiting this moment, this invitation, for all of my life.

Song of Songs 2, Psalm 32:7, Zephaniah 3:17, Exodus 15, Exodus 17, Isaiah 54, Genesis 22, Isaiah 40, Isaiah 54, Isaiah 55, Isaiah 35, Psalms 32, & 52, Psalms 94, Romans 8, Isaiah 43, 1 Corinthians 2:9

Deeper Still
Chapter 2, Inviting Love

1. Zephaniah 3:17 says, "He will take great delight in you; in His love He will no longer rebuke you but will rejoice over you with singing." It is clear He sings songs over us. Ask Him to allow you to hear His love song to you. Write down what you hear.

2. Is it difficult to believe that nothing can keep His love from you? If yes, why? What lies are creating distance between you and Jesus? Journal about the roadblocks you feel are hindering you from experiencing His love. Ask Him to penetrate these obstructions with His goodness, glory and mercy.

3. Are there areas of your life where you feel ashamed to let Him in? Can you pinpoint what they are?

4. Are there former things you need to forget and move past? Ask Jesus to show you the new things He is growing and maturing in and for you. Can you see it? Do you believe it? As a prophetic act, sit outside and listen to the birds sing. Prophesy the old, unfruitful winter is over, and your new season has begun.

5. Where have little foxes invaded your garden and hindered your relationship with Jesus? Do you know what they are? If not, ask Him.

PERSONAL LOVE NOTE TO JESUS

HOLY PILLOW TALK

Personal Love Note to Jesus

Chapter 3
HEALING LOVE

What You Might Experience . . .

Chapter Three pinpoints distractions that may stop you from accepting Jesus' invitation for deeper intimacy. It uncovers any areas where cleansing and healing are needed from generational sins and ungodly beliefs. Soul and spirit wounds will be exposed. Be thorough as you release forgiveness towards others and receive forgiveness for yourself.

Do not rush through this chapter. Take your time and fully focus on repenting for every detour in your heart, renouncing and revoking the grip of each lie. Allow your mind to be changed. Truly, you can encounter Him and take hold of the lasting freedom of His healing love.

What Others Experienced . . .

> "This chapter walks through breaking and renouncing any chains you are weighted by. Some of the descriptions did not pertain to me, but some did. Saying them aloud, as well as audibly declaring freedom from them made me feel lighter, strengthened, and more assured of my walk with Jesus."

"This was my favorite chapter! It made me want to dig deeper, removing the cobwebs from every room and corner of my life, the places where I needed His touch to bring healing."

"I never thought about "forgiving God." This was eye-opening for me. I've always just distanced myself and then asked Him to forgive me. This cycle became my habit. This chapter opened up another part of my heart. Deep healing took place within me."

THE BRIDE SPEAKS:

I am in the middle of a dark, sleepless night. I lay restlessly on my bed, thinking about You.

I feel a distance between us.

Where are You? Where did You go? What have I done?

I feel the darkness all around me. It is devastating to experience void where You once surrounded me. I said I wanted to come away with You, yet I lingered. I became distracted, and my distraction led to procrastination. I am beginning to see that my delay allowed this void between us.

I did this to me. I did this to You. I did this to us.

Forgive me, Jesus.

My foolish inhibitions and lack of trust interrupted our bond. Why did I withdraw? Am I scared? What am I scared of?

I say I want to come deeper into You, but my actions speak differently. You say nothing could ever separate our union, but my disobedience has tried to limit Your faithfulness.

Every second of distance between us feels like an hour. I cannot go on like this. I am in need, yet again.

I have been shaken and brought to my senses. I need Your Presence more than Your presents, for You *are* my blessing. I crave Your constant closeness above an occasional encounter. I see now how our intimacy, through prayer and communion, is the only platform I ever need to seek. I have reached for the prestige of earth and found it fleeting.

Now I see it clearly:

Sitting at Your feet is the highest seat, the strongest posture, the deepest place of influence.

I am not whole, apart from You. The pain of feeling disconnected from You is devastating.

My heart is crushed.

I feel abandoned and alone. These are the effects of my decision to linger and not come away with You when You asked. I treated Your beautiful love invitation as common and familiar.

Forgive me.

Please ask me to come away with You again.

This time, my pursuit of Your invitation will bring You joy! I will abandon this childish cycle, this toxic self-centered pattern. Let a roar, a cry, a groan be birthed and released within me, and may it break this cycle and destroy this pattern. Jesus, come and peel back another layer of my heart.

I give You full permission. Awaken my sound!
Help me find my voice!

Let the first word of my awakened voice be a forever "yes," and may the first acts of Your love on my heart deal with the broken roots in me.

According to Your unfailing love, have mercy on me. Because of Your great compassion, blot out my transgressions and the stains of my sins.

HOLY PILLOW TALK

Your blood is my only atonement. Life is found in Your blood. Wash away all my iniquity and guilt. Purify me completely.

Forgive me, Jesus. Forgive me. I repent!

You desire truth in the inner part of me. You want light to shine on my darkness. May the Spirit of Truth illuminate that which is displeasing to You.

I invite You into the hidden places. Teach me Your wisdom and Your truth. Circumcise my heart with the sword of Your word. Give me a heart of flesh for my heart of stone.

Empty out of my heart every false substance. Make every crooked thing straight and brighten every dark way with Your light.

Come, Spirit of Truth!

Purify me and I will be clean; wash me until I am pure in heart.

I confess all my mistakes to You. Remove hypocrisy from my heart. I am overjoyed to be cleansed and made pure. Your sacrifice is the only thing that could ever create this new, unstained heart within me.

Grant me a willing spirit to sustain me. Fill me with pure thoughts and desires.

I choose to think on whatever is true and honorable, right, and pure, lovely, and admirable.

I will think about things that are excellent and worthy of praise.

I will think about You. I will meditate on Who You are, what You have done and what You are going to do.

Apply Your atoning blood and wash away my sins and family curses. Uproot flawed beliefs. Heal any wounds and memories attached to:

- Disease & Infirmities
- Abandonment
- Abuse & Neglect
- Control
- Grief & Loss
- Disappointment
- Jealousy & Envy
- Unworthiness
- Depression
- Torment
- Self-pity
- Isolation
- Idolatry
- Rejection & Betrayal
- Divorce
- Poverty & Debt
- Addiction
- Passivity
- Violence & Murder
- Injustice
- Blocked Intimacy
- Forgetfulness
- Laziness
- Illegitimacy
- Rebellion
- Judgment
- Doubt & Unbelief
- Anger
- Greed
- Infidelity
- Obsessiveness
- Pride
- Inferiority
- Pornography
- Shame
- Deception
- Striving & Performance
- Disobedience
- Manipulation
- Condemnation
- Religion & Legalism
- Suspicion
- Strife
- Bitterness
- Double-mindedness
- Mental Illness
- Fear & Anxiety
- Fatigue
- Mocking
- Witchcraft & Occult
- Intimidation
- Confusion
- Enabling
- Laziness
- Competition
- Resentment
- Nervousness
- Perversion & Sexual Sin

Jesus, in Your justice, powerfully resolve the conflicts in me. Deal with my trust issues! Deal with my disappointment! Deal with my unbelief! Deal with my hope deferred! Deal with all negativity, and every emotional blockage and baggage.

Examine me for generational sins and iniquities, ungodly beliefs, and unresolved traumas that keep me from You.

None of these are too difficult for Your love.

I want Your reign in me to be absolute, so I slow down to truly explore my heart with You.

I know complete freedom in these areas is my birthright, so please do whatever You must to establish me in Your freedom.

Do whatever it takes to restore my alignment to You. I am willing to do my part and I know You are faithful to do Yours. I repent for aligning myself with any spirit other than Holy Spirit.

I repent for agreeing with my emotions and letting them rule over me.

I repent for the places and decisions where I departed from Your Presence.

I renounce my agreement with every generational sin, ungodly belief, toxic thought, wicked stronghold, and unhealthy emotion. I dismantle them in Your Truth. I revoke their ability to impact or influence my spirit, soul, and body any further.

By the power of Your name, I break the soul ties I have made with corrupted emotions, and I forbid them to operate in my life from this day forward.

I dismantle and destroy the soul ties I have made with people, places and possessions that have led me away from You. I cancel their influence on any facet of my life.

Heal all the traumatic, tormenting memories of my past. Interrupt the continuing loop of pain and confusion in my mind. I open myself to let go of unforgiveness and bitterness, and to relearn the thoughts of wholeness.

I forgive those who have sinned against me and those who influenced me to sin. I forgive those who have used me and abused me. I release them for what they have done to me or said about me.

I also forgive myself now in Your powerful name, Jesus.

The same grace I extend to others, I receive for myself.

If my unforgiveness has given the enemy legal right to inflict my body, mind, will, emotions or spirit in any way, his authority is now revoked. Jesus, Your broken body and spilled blood have cancelled out his assignments against me. As I watch Your victory take its place in my life, I am undone.

As I have forgiven and will continue to forgive, I claim my total healing.

There is now nothing missing or broken in my life. Be free, mind, body, and spirit!

You have done the impossible. Your love is alive, and I take hold of the freedom Your broken body and spilled blood bought for me!

I am whole because of You, Jesus! Thank You!

Finally, I release forgiveness to You. I have blamed You for my pain and disappointment.

I'm sorry.

I have met You. I know You are good. No matter how circumstances may seem, You are good, and You love me. You have a purpose and a plan for me, and I can trust You completely.

Lover, as You examine my heart, I know You see my fear of intimacy with You. Forgive me. I don't even know how or when this formed. I just know I want to be free from it.

I open to You every door that has been closed in my heart. I feel vulnerable and exposed in this new, intimate place, but I trust You to be gentle and kind. I choose to no longer hide my mess from You. I fall completely into Your trustworthy arms; avoiding You has been exhausting.

I will not resist Your pursuit of my heart any longer.
I give in. I let go. I surrender all to You, Jesus!

The promise You made to me has taken root in my heart. You take my ashes and turn them into a crown of beauty. You gather my tears of mourning and give me the oil of blissful joy and gladness. You give me a mantle of extravagant praise and discard my garment of heaviness of failure and fear.

I gladly step out of the dark storm of troubles and the whirlwind of emotions, being found in Your light and healing. Your light is my life. The pain I have endured from our separation has developed bravery and boldness within me. It is just like You to work even the darkness for my good. I am unshakeable as I focus my attention on You.

Even if the storms continue to rage all around me, I remain still and at peace.

As I answer Your call to walk on the water and dance on the

waves, I know You hold my hand and will not let go. These storms are created to drive me to my destination more quickly. You said we would go to the other side and I believe You.

The enemy intends to overwhelm me and drown me in turbulence, but You have designed the storms to expedite me toward Your promises and destiny for me. I will be still knowing Your promises are backed by the honor of Your name.

Therefore, I choose to welcome the storm as your prophetic words hasten to me. As long I as gaze into Your eyes, I will not be overcome with fear. I will not drown. You are the Master of the wind. You are the One who speaks peace.

You are my anchor of hope and I am secure.

I know what I must do. I must search for and seek after You with all of my heart. I choose to pursue You fully. I simply cannot live without You. I will search high and low to find You, my true Love.

As the deer longs for flowing streams of water, so I long for You.

I thirst for You. You are my only desire. I love You more than any other. The deep within me cries out to the deep within You. I know now that nothing else can satisfy me. You promise when I chase after You, I will find You. I am coming after You with all of me!

I called out, and You came running to my rescue. You entered my wilderness and took me in Your strong arms. Who is like You, Lord?

I fasten my heart to Yours and will not let go again. Together we are ascending from the wilderness, hand in hand. The place of pain and regret is far behind me now. Your glory cloud has enveloped me.

Even in the wilderness, Your grace reached me. I was matured, marked by how much I need You. I learned resilience and resolve. I became hungry for You, and my hunger drove me home.

As I learned Who You are in the wilderness, joyful confidence took deep root within me. Patient endurance refined my character, leading me to hope without fear of disappointment. I experienced Your endless love.

Your patient love has ruined me. I am baptized in Your aroma of frankincense and myrrh. What once was bitter within me is now sweet, and all that was defiled is now pure.

My time with You is most precious. I pour out my worship on You, and You pour out Your Presence on me. What a beautiful transaction! I am lost for words.

My tears drench Your feet with thankfulness and gratitude. You consume my thoughts. Your fragrance on me is the smell of unity, and it makes me smile with confident joy.

Surrounded by angelic warriors, I ride with You in the Father's marriage chariot. This unseen, undefeated, unstoppable army protects me from enemies of the past, present, and future, ensuring that our wedding day will not be delayed or derailed. These Heavenly experts of war are armed for battle and trained for combat.

All of Heaven fights for us.

Together, You and I sit on the seat called "Mercy," the place of authority You built for us. Founded upon Your sacrificial love, this throne will never decay.

Jesus, You are dressed and expectant for our wedding day. How handsome You are! I never knew I could love or be loved like this. You wear Your crown and I wear my spotless gown. My heart is full and bursting with overwhelming anticipation.

You take my breath away!

JESUS, MY BRIDEGROOM RESPONDS:

In the midst of your struggle, I was always with you. I heard your cry for help. You were never alone. I felt your pain. I walked with you. Do not think for a moment that I was not watching out for you, Lovely One.

Your deep wounds are now healed, the scars a beautiful testimony of what our love can do. They remind you to be thankful, not filled with shame and regret. Now you know My heart for you is filled with love. Your pain has drawn you closer to Me.

My love will not abandon or reject you, so do not fear. I Am not going anywhere. You cannot possibly cause Me to leave you.

I Am for you, not against you.

All I have belongs to you.

We will write a new love story, together, you and Me.

I will help and protect you. I will guard and guide you. I will not let you stumble or fall. I Am directing your steps. You are not forgotten or ignored. I Am always watching you. My eyes are always open, and always looking out for you. I Am guarding you from calamity, danger, and evil.

You are safe with Me.

Now, take My hand and dance with Me. We will celebrate how you have been set free by My healing love.

Ezekiel 36, Proverbs 8, Psalms 51, Luke 3, Philippians 4, Isaiah 61, Proverbs 30, Psalm 42, Romans 5, Psalm 121, Mark 4, Psalm 138, Psalm 46

HOLY PILLOW TALK

Deeper Still
Chapter 3, Healing Love

1. What distractions have led you to procrastination, resulting in disobedience? Have you noticed a cycle the enemy subtly uses to bring distractions into your life? When/How does it first begin?

2. From the detailed list of characteristics on page 60, what wounds resonated with you, specifically? Have you observed any of these in your immediate or extended family? Have they also been evident in your life? If yes, treat this soberly. Slow down and go through the process of repenting, renouncing, and revoking until you sense a release in your spirit.

3. Who do you need to forgive? Call out their name to Jesus and ask Him to help you truly and completely forgive them.

4. Take a few moments and thank Him for the wilderness. Thank Him for His closeness and Presence. Don't forget to thank Him for the pain, which brought you closer to Him.

5. Recall a time when Jesus walked with you through a tough season. Ask Him to show you where He held your hand as you walked on the troubled waters together.

Personal Love Note to Jesus

HOLY PILLOW TALK

Personal Love Note to Jesus

Chapter 4
FRUITFUL LOVE

What You Might Experience...

Chapter Four will challenge you to grow with Holy Spirit, partnering together to bring forth the fruit of maturity in your life. Yet one thing remains: to experience and express the brilliant life of His resurrection, we must first accept and embrace His proposal.

He is the Bridegroom, and we the beloved one who offers our yes.

Consider what it truly means to say yes to Jesus as you meditate on all His descriptive and holy names.

What Others Experienced...

> "In declaring Jesus' attributes in this chapter, I felt a secure peace come over me. 'Captain, Teacher, Rescuer...' Yes! I cried, knowing as I declared these words, I was bringing delight to Him. I was created to praise Him, and this chapter is a springboard into adoration."

> "The words of this chapter made me feel very seen and very loved by Him. I felt my capacity to know Him more expanding within me."

"Hearing Him propose to me and asking me to come away with Him made me weep. I am understanding the deeper my love grows, the better our communication gets. He is so intentional!"

JESUS, MY BRIDEGROOM SPEAKS:

I find such pleasure simply sitting and admiring you.

You are the epitome of beauty! Your eyes sparkle with passion for Me. My gaze is fixed on you and cannot be removed. One look from you is all it takes.

I cherish you! You are My favorite!

I see your undying devotion for Me, a new bud on My vine. You have tasted of Me and have become ready to surrender all. You are learning to trust Me. Your life has become clean and pure. You have been washed in My Word. Grace and holiness are your perfume. Steadfastness and truth are found within you. Virtue and faith reside in your heart.

You are truly My delight.

Your lips are fiery, burning red, for I have put the white-hot coal from My altar to your lips. Your guilt and sin are washed away.

Now the words you speak are a refreshing spring. From you, I receive indescribable pleasure. I see your humble, open heart of love, filled with yearning desire for Me. It is undeniable.

When I look at you, I see your confidence. You are secure in who you are because you know Who I Am. No one defines you but Me. You are who I say you are. Your identity is found in My Father and in Me, because My Father and I are One. I am in Him. He is in Me. We are in *you*.

There is nothing impossible for Us.

Now, answer me, My Love. Will you come away with Me? Will you let Me sweep you off your feet? Will you be Mine and make Me your own?

Will you enter into this covenant of love with Me?

Will you be My Bride?

The Bride responds:

I have determined to be with You no matter what. I must go away to the mountaintop with You, despite any residue of fear that may attempt to linger within me.

I have realized now: all I need to do is say, "Yes." You will handle the rest.

Whatever may try to stop me must bow down to Who You are. The distracting voice of the enemy is silenced when I whisper Your most powerful and precious name.

There is nothing and no one more powerful than You.

Going deeper is the only thing that matters now. I did not know I was hungry until I tasted of You. I did not know I was thirsty until I drank of Your love. To fully know You and be known by You is my one desire.

I continually ache to grasp Your wonders more fully. I want to experience Your resurrection power as it flows into me and works in, through and around me.

I must become thoroughly acquainted with every aspect of Who You are, in Your brilliant life and even in Your suffering. I choose to die to myself, to my flesh, over and over again. In this death experience, I am continually conformed to Your likeness and our oneness is made complete.

I have considered and weighed the price of being Your Bride. Nothing is better than You. Even if it costs me everything, You are worth it. All my desires are satisfied in You.

So, I cry out in a loud voice:

"Yes! I will be Your Bride!"

HOLY PILLOW TALK

JESUS, MY BRIDEGROOM RESPONDS:

Do you realize I see you without blemish or flaw?

Your bridal gown is spotless and white.

I know you are ready to journey to the higher peaks, leaving behind the hideaway of previous comfort zones and false securities, and abandoning the wilderness seclusion. I have prepared an adventure for us!

Let us slow dance under the covering of covenant faith. Our chuppah is beautifully decorated with ivory, silk, and cascading flowers.

We make our vows and seal our covenant here.

Afterward, we look down from the mountain peaks where our sanctuary rests. Our place of communion is your seat of authority with Me. I have raised you up and seated you with Me in the Heavens. You belong here. This is where we wage war and win against the thief who wants to kill, steal, and destroy.

I dwell within you. Gain the fullness of this revelation, My Love. I dwell, live, and reside in you. My Spirit imparts life to you because You are fully accepted by My Father. The same power that raised Me from the dead lives in you! You are complete in Me and My fullness overflows within you.

We live in unity together; all I have is yours. This is what covenant looks like.

Listen while I tell you the way you make Me feel.

I Am held captive by your heart. With one glance of your eyes, I

Am completely undone. I see you smile as you meditate on Me. Your expression makes My day. Knowing I Am in your thoughts brings Me indescribable bliss!

You have stolen My affection. You have won My attention. Every moment of every day, you leave Me breathless.

This is what you were made for: intimacy with Me.

I am enraptured when you incline your ear to listen to the rhythm of My heartbeat. You hear it even now, steady and strong.

Your lavish worship propels you into new, refreshing rivers of My glory. Piece by piece, I Am uncovering more of Myself to you. Your desire for Me brings Me ecstasy. You have ravished My heart because I know you are desperately in love with Me!

When I was breaking My Body and spilling My Blood, you were on my mind. Thinking of you drove me to put the cup to My lips. I asked my Father to take it from Me, but there was no other way to free you.

I drank it willingly, and I thought of you the whole time.

When I was betrayed, I saw you. I thought of you. I love you.

In the garden, I saw you. I thought of you. I love you.

When I was beaten, I saw you. I thought of you. I love you.

On Calvary, I saw you. I thought of you. I love you.

During every part of the process, I saw you. I thought of you. I love you.

HOLY PILLOW TALK

What helped me endure it? I focused on this moment between you and Me. I thought of this intimate love we would cultivate .

You were worth it.

Every ounce of pain I suffered was worth the intimacy we share. I submitted to My Father in the garden and drank the cup for you.

Now, Beloved, you have become My garden.

Within you is where I dwell.

Because of you, the garden of pressing, tears, pain and sacrifice has now become a garden of pleasure, treasure, passion, and satisfaction.

You are My pleasure and My treasure.

You are My passion and My satisfaction.

You are My garden. I find all of this in you. Thank you for opening yourself to Me.

Your love is far more pleasing than a fine wine – simply intoxicating! You are My poetry. Your sweet praise stuns Me. I can feel your love for Me. Your kisses are as sweet as honey from the honeycomb. I savor all your worship. It is like fresh air to Me. Your words release milk and honey. They please Me.

You are My Promised Land.

You are My private paradise, My gorgeous garden of delight. You are only open to Me, closed to all others. You are My secret spring and pure fountain. Your inward life is sprouting up, bringing forth a harvest.

You are growing and maturing. I smell the aroma of My Spirit's delectable fruit, growing within you:

Unfailing Love

Overflowing Joy

Invincible Peace

Enduring Patience

Relentless Kindness

Abiding Goodness

Overcoming Faithfulness

Tangible Gentleness

Steadfast Self-Control

Your life flows into Mine, pure as a garden spring.

There is a deep well within you, Beloved. Remove the cap and push past your former limits. Is there something holding you back? Whatever it is, bring it to Me. We can handle it together.

Now it the time for My rivers of living water to burst out from within you, flowing from your innermost being!

The Bride responds:

I am compelled to share my heart with You, even though You already know everything in me. You told me You would help me, so I am choosing to trust You.

I am embarrassed to admit there have been times I have been jealous of the successes and victories of others. I have compared myself to them. I have even found myself in competition with them.

I am sorry, Jesus. These feelings have capped Your rivers from flowing freely within me. The plague of comparison has robbed me of joy, sleep, and peace.

I ask You to forgive me and free me from jealousy, comparison, and competition. I am finished with trying to be like someone else. I want to be who You created me to be. I want to fulfill what You have destined for my life.

Let the rushing river of Your Spirit flood my being. A trickling stream is not enough. Ankle-deep, knee-deep, even waist-deep water is too shallow. I want a river deep enough to swim in. May Your river within me flow, making salty waters fresh and pure. Bring life and abundance everywhere I go.

When I live in union with You, producing a harvest of fruit is not difficult. You are my source. When I focus on You, there is no limit on my life. It is not a struggle to be who You created me to be.

You are the Fountainhead of my life.

Fruitfulness surges from within me when I live in covenant unity with You.

I declare Your powerful words are alive in me. They are in my mouth. I can ask whatever I desire, and You will do it.

My life bears abundant fruit, demonstrating I am mature in You. My thoughts, words, actions, and reactions prove You have been cultivating good fruit in me. You are the vine, and I am the branch. I produce great harvest, because I yield to the pruning process.

I am intimately joined to You. You are always caring and watching out for me.

Thank You, Jesus.

I have known You as:

Redeemer, Comforter, and Friend

Revelator, Perfector, and Pursuer

Revealer, Yahweh, and Purifier

Savior, Healer and Warrior

Shepherd, Counselor, and Restorer

Creator, Sustainer, and Emmanuel

Sanctifier, Deliverer, and Jehovah

Preserver, Giver, and Fountain

Shield, Servant, and Keeper

Captain, Teacher, and Rescuer

Provider, Elohim, and Master

Adonai, Mediator, and Commander

Friend, Refiner, and Comforter

Breaker, Rhema and Logos

Messiah, Carpenter, and Guide

Foundation, Supplier, and Advocate

Defender, King, and Lord

Overcomer, Ruler, and Multiplier

Rewarder, Hero, and Priest

Liberator, Judge, and Watchman

Conqueror, Majesty, and Fortress

Intercessor, Artist, and Visionary

Lamb, Lion, and Cornerstone

Son, Plumb line, and Confidant

Forgiver, Pioneer, and Offering

Reformer, Rabbi, and Reviver

Author, Finisher, and Refuge

Anointer, Alpha, and Omega

Baptizer, Contender, and Dreamer

Sacrifice, River, and Prophet

Well, Reconciler, and Activator

Justifier, Vindicator, and Encourager

Avenger, Rock, and Champion

Branch, Root, and Vine

But now, I know you as

Lover.

This is my most favorite.

I long to make You known. I live to declare Who You are.

All You have done for me and in me is miraculous.

You are worthy of my life.
You are worthy of my uninterrupted focus.

You brought me from death to life. I am awestruck by Your goodness to me. You are altogether lovely. You fascinate me.

How is it that the One Who spoke galaxies into existence loves me so? I confess I do not understand Your holy obsession for me.

Would You help me understand? I want to grasp it.

May Your awakening breath continually blow upon my life. Awaken any part of me that still lies dormant. I want to be fully alive and fully Yours.

Stir me!

Breathe upon me with Your Spirit! Come, O breath of God, from the four winds! Wake up, North Wind! Swirl, South Wind! Come alive, East Wind! Break open, West Wind! Blow upon my garden with the wind of Your Spirit! Flow from the four corners of the earth!

I have seen what You can do. Nothing is impossible for You. Make every area of me alive again with the kiss of Your lips.

Your kisses are electrifying. Your gaze is penetrating. Your voice is mesmerizing. Your touch is tantalizing. Your face is captivating. Your breath is rejuvenating.

I can't resist You, nor do I want to.

Never stop stirring up Your Presence within me. Spare nothing as You tend me, Your fruitful garden of love. I hold nothing back. I am drenched in the fragrance of Your attention.

Come walk with me. Talk deeply with me. Tell me I belong to You. I am Your own.

Experience the fruit of Your life and power within me. Our love is fruitful. May every step I take toward You bring You joy.

Song of Songs 4, John 15, Ezekiel 37, Luke 1, Isaiah 6, John 10, John 15, Philippians 3, Ephesians 2, Romans 8, Colossians 2, John 7, Galatians 5, Zechariah 6

DEEPER STILL
Chapter 4, Fruitful Love

1. Is it difficult to hear Him speak so intimately about how He sees you? If yes, what specific part makes you most uncomfortable? Journal about it here. Ask Him to let you see yourself through His eyes.

2. Is there an absence of fruitfulness in your life? List three fruit of the Spirit needing further maturity in you. Ask Jesus to help you cultivate these areas.

3. From the list of the names of Jesus on pages 86-87, which five names do you most identify with?

4. From the same list, which five names do you crave to experience as reality in your life? List those names here, searching out correlating Scripture references to build your understanding and your faith. Call on Him aloud.

5. Take a few minutes to look up an old hymn entitled, "In The Garden." *(1913,* C. Austin Miles.) Close your eyes and listen to the words of this prophetically romantic song. Release your imagination to picture yourself walking and talking with Jesus.

PERSONAL LOVE NOTES TO JESUS

HOLY PILLOW TALK

Personal Love Notes to Jesus

Chapter 5
LUKEWARM LOVE

What You Might Experience...

Chapter Five may possibly be the most difficult chapter to navigate. Recognizing and unmasking the compromise or complacency in our lives can be devastating. This chapter addresses lukewarm areas in your love for Jesus. Be sure to take your time, allowing these words to free you from your place of stagnation, while setting your heart ablaze for Him. Allow extra time to tell Him Who He is to you. You may find yourself raising your voice in praise, declaring His glorious attributes!

What Others Experienced...

> "Chapter 5 was difficult to get through. It walks you through fully relinquishing yourself to Jesus, even the parts you want to keep for yourself, or pieces you want to hide. The openness that comes with allowing Him all access, even the ugly parts, creates an irresistible connection."

> "I was reminded that relationships must be cultivated, even with the Bridegroom. I realized that sometimes I get a bit slack in that department."

"This chapter convicted me, which I am grateful for! I never saw myself as complacent. Yet His love is never lukewarm, so mine must not be either. I definitely sense a new fiery love for Him. I think this was my favorite chapter!"

His Bride Speaks:

Jesus, my love for You has grown cool.

I am not sure when it happened, but the roaring flame has faded to lukewarm embers and my devotion has fallen asleep. Spiritual sluggishness and apathy have permeated my heart.

The days of our honeymoon have ended, and my passion has waned. My desire for You has faded.

I feel lethargic toward You. I hate this feeling, this sluggish thickness in my soul, these dry swallows of dust. It has been too long since I have taken a drink from Your springs of life.

The world's desires crept into me and I became cozy with complacency. I befriended lukewarm living. I compromised and chose convenience over You, my Bridegroom.

For a moment I thought I had it all figured out, and in my deception, I took my gaze off You. Pride snuck into my heart. I am sickened by my haughty thoughts and wretched stagnation.

I need You, only.
How did I forget that?

I had a dream about us. You were coming to me in the dark. Suddenly Your romantic singing caught my attention and awakened my soul. I heard You knock at my heart's door, pleading with me to open to You.

You said to me,

"Arise, My Love. Open your heart deeper still to Me.

"There is no one else I desire but you. I need you to leave this place of slumber, this bed of comfort. Come be with Me tonight. I need to spend time with you. I desire your company. You bring Me great joy and pleasure. I need you.

"My flawless one, will you get up now? Will you leave slumber and lukewarmness? Do you lack the strength to be alert? Are you unable to stay awake with Me, even for one hour? Can you not keep your eyes open?

"I see that your spirit is eager, but your flesh is weak.

"I have prayed to My Father for you. I asked Him to help you fasten His Word firmly to your heart, that you would joyfully receive and carry His Word well. Because of My deep love for you, I asked Him by the power of My name to protect, keep and watch over you. I prayed that you would experience and enter into the delight the Father and I share.

"I believe He will overflow you with strength and peace and guard your heart from all evil. By the truth of His Word, He has set you apart as holy. You have been commissioned to represent Us. I asked My Father to help you live a life fully dedicated by experiencing the love He and I share. It is your inheritance to dwell as One with Us.

"My Beloved, I Am always praying and interceding for you. So is Holy Spirit.

We both intercede to the Father for you daily."

HOLY PILLOW TALK

As I experienced this dream of You and me, my love was rekindled. As slumber gives way to clarity, Your name arises on my lips.

Jesus, thank You for interceding to the Father for me. I need Your help. I ask that You continually show me my wrong ways, sinful thoughts, and unholy behavior. I do not want to be lukewarm. I want to be fervent with passion.

Forgive me! You made me clean, but I became comfortable and complacent. I chose me over You. I chose my flesh over Your Spirit. Convenience became my bed, but I refuse to stay there. I refuse to be lulled to sleep again. I will stay awakened.

Increase my hunger! Satisfy my thirst! Make my passion for You greater than my desire for comfort!

Your sacrifice on the cross purchased my white garment, removing my shame and disgrace. You have cleansed my life and made me new and clean, giving me a brilliant and priceless mantle.

Guide me to identify and eliminate anything that distracts me from You. You are worth every ounce of my focus. Reveal to me what does not belong in my life. I ran after other lovers that brought only temporary fulfillment. I cheated myself from experiencing Your power, peace, and Presence.

Yet You have remained faithful, even when I was not. You are my loyal, long-suffering Lover.

Forgive me for the idols I have built and have become fixated on.
Forgive me for the idols I have boasted about.
Forgive me for the idols my itching ears have been drawn to.
Forgive me for neglecting You when I allowed my mind to become cluttered with worthless thoughts and empty fascinations.

Forgive me for being shallow and self-centered, for pushing my own agenda instead of Yours.

Forgive the unholy affairs I have had with the world, caught up in the lusts of my flesh, lusts of my eyes, and the pride in my life.

I can feel Your life filling me all over again, as I humbly let Your light fall on my waywardness.

Quiet the noise in my mind and the lies in my ear. Silence the voices that compete for the full attention that belongs to You. Mute the negativity that tries to overtake me.

I want to be a Bride of complete devotion.

Strip away anything that dulls my affection for You.
Strip away every thief that steals my time with You.
Strip away opportunities that would initiate compromise.
Strip away relationships that push my intimacy with You to lower rank.
Strip away detours that would lead my eyes astray.

I want to be ablaze with passion, not frozen in apathy or lukewarm with complacency. Burn away stagnation and lethargy. Mark me with Your name. Brand Your signature upon my heart.

I belong to You. No other lover has my attention or affection.

You are everything!

Riches, wealth and fame are nothing. The comforts of this world are futile in comparison to You. My life cannot be measured by anything except my covenant bond with You, Jesus.

Apart from You, I am miserable, poor, blind, barren, and naked! With You, I am elated, rich, sharp, fruitful, and clothed.

HOLY PILLOW TALK

I find all I need in You.

I exhale, emptying my being of distraction and compromise.

And now, I inhale You in, fully and vibrantly. My lungs roar and I am alive and alert. You are the air I breathe, and You never run out.

I welcome Your rebuke and guidance, My Bridegroom. I know it is offered in love and meant for my good. I am eager to pursue holiness and to live a fully consecrated life with You.

Anoint my eyes with salve so I can fully see You. Do not allow blindness to darken my heart. Point out deception and pride when they convince me to be self-sufficient. I know I need You. I am zealous to take off the masks that have hindered me from seeing all of You. Restore my vision.

Revive the wonder I once had for You. I want to see Your beauty. I want to look at You as if I have never seen You before. I release every false, fleshly expectation of how You will move in my life.

Instead, I am filled with a spirit of expectancy.

So, come! Walk with me however You want to.

I am wide open.

Knock again on the door of my heart. I am eager to hear Your voice, anxiously anticipating our time together. Reach into me and unlock me. I invite You to put Your hand on my heart and unlatch me completely. I tremble at Your tender, intimate touch.

I am awakened and open for more of You.

My holy surrender presses Your sweet fragrance into my skin.

What was lukewarm within me is renewed ablaze when You speak to me. As You touch me, the miracle of Your loving affection sets every frozen fiber of me afire. My stiff heart melts when I look into Your flaming eyes.

Come into me. Let us feast on one another. May You find pleasure within me. Train my love to grow white hot, never dwindling to lukewarmness again.

Only You deserve my adoration. Only You are worthy of my focus. I let go of all that interferes with my pursuit of You.

I totally surrender.

There is nothing more important than You. I am ruined for anything else.

I choose to seek You with renewed, wholehearted devotion because I want fresh fellowship with You. I cannot be satisfied with anything less.

I am coming after You! I will seek You and I will find You. This is Your promise to me. I will call to You and You will answer me and tell me great, unsearchable, remarkable, hidden secrets that I have never heard or known before.

There are some who do not understand our love. They have settled for a past memory and old experiences with You. They carry a hint of Your fragrance, but it is fading and stale. Because I have chosen not to settle on yesterday's encounter with You, they have rejected, harassed, and mistreated me.

Even still, I will persist even when I am misunderstood. When my passion for You leads me through persecution, I will hold Your Presence as my reward.

Some have asked; Why I care for You so deeply? Are there not other loves, other paths with similar mystical benefit that would require less of me? Why am I so loyal to Your way, Your eyes, Your Word? How did You steal away my heart? What kind of love is this?

My answer to them is simple:

"He loved me first."

You are by far better than any other, far above all comparison. You glow with exquisite, handsome beauty, yet You are completely approachable. You give me full access to all of You.

I completely trust and follow Your leadership. You are all-knowing and all-powerful.

I always have more than enough with You. You provide me a place to rest, taking me to the streams of peace. This is the place where You restore and revive me. You open for me paths of righteousness, leading me in Your footsteps as I bring honor and glory to Your name.

I understand that even when unknown, unfamiliar paths appear before my feet, You guide me. Even through valleys of darkness, I boldly tread all fear underfoot, for it was under Your feet first.

You will never forsake me. No, You will lead me all the way through to the end. Your authority is my strength, peace, and comfort.

Your perfect love drives out all my fear. I will never be lonely for I am never alone. You are always with me.

When my enemies rise up against me, I dauntlessly feast on You in their presence. You are my bread and wine. You anoint me with the fragrance of Your Holy Spirit. As I drink You in, my cup is continually filled to overflowing. As I feast on You, I find unending pleasure.

I refuse to fear the future; Your goodness and love are in hot pursuit of me. I will be with You forever! I am Your favorite!

You are altogether lovely. Your hair is white like wool, like glistening snow. You are called the Ancient of Days because You are full of all wisdom, righteousness, and justice. Your face shines like lightning and Your eyes are like flames of fire, penetrating like torches. Your garments are pure, white linen. A gold belt is around Your waist, and a regal, gold crown is on Your head. Your body looks like it has been sculpted from precious, rare stones. Your arms and feet glisten like polished bronze, as though they were glowing in a fire.

Your voice is deep and resonant, the full echo of many waters. You sound like the voices of many sons and daughters who are being transformed into Your likeness. Your voice thunders, and rumblings come from Your mouth. When You roar, it resounds with majestic force, brilliantly bright. Your symphonic sound echoes through the skies and seas, fracturing forests, moving mountains, and splintering summits. None can withstand the might of Your shout.

Your voice sounds like hope.

No one speaks words so anointed as You! Your words pierce and heal me, leaving me expectant to hear more from You.

Your hands hold unlimited power, revealing Your holiness and majestic glory. You are steadfast in all You do. Your ways are the ways of righteousness, founded in truth and authority. Nothing and nobody can contend with You.

Therefore, I fear nothing, for You are my Kinsman-Redeemer. You are for me. You will rescue me. You call me by my name, and I am Yours.

When I pass through the deep, stormy sea, I know You will be there with me.

When I walk through raging rivers, I will not drown.

When I tread through persecution like fiery flames, I will not be burned. The flames will not harm me for You are walking in the fire with me.

You are my Way Maker, and Path Director. You light up the pathway that leads me to abundant life, and my feet will never slip.

You are the source of my salvation. Fear has lost its hold on me. My heart will not be afraid because You are with me, and I will not be shaken.

Jesus, I seek only one thing from You... To dwell with You, looking on Your beautiful face and basking in Your glory is what I desire.

The only place I want to be is with You.

Your whispers of love are the sweetest sound that exists. You are absolutely delightful. There is none like You. Everything about You fills me with holy desire. Your words are sweeter than honey in my mouth.

With You, I have everything. Without You, I have nothing.

Even when I am not faithful to You, You are faithful to me. You are never apathetic towards me, for not a sliver of Your nature is lukewarm. Thank You for never leaving or forsaking me. I am never without You.

Truly, You are my best friend. Your relentless love for me compels You toward me, as though you consider me irresistible. You are lovesick for me. I am Your adored and adorned Bride.

I set before my eyes the fullness of Who You are:

You are hope. You are faithful. You are constant.
You are priceless. You are unshakeable. You are unchanging.
You are unfailing. You are flawless. You are fascinating.
You are invincible. You are good. You are joy.
You are selfless. You are revival. You are elation.
You are untameable. You are steady. You are humble.
You are glorified. You are sovereign. You are paradise.
You are fire. You are jealous. You are consuming.
You are undefeated. You are balm. You are provision.
You are truth. You are excellent. You are loyal.
You are alive. You are innocent. You are awakening.
You are uncontainable. You are amazing. You are powerful.
You are holy. You are righteous. You are faultless.
You are matchless. You are worthy. You are almighty.
You are perfection. You are royalty. You are magnificent.

You are pleasure. You are handsome. You are kind.
You are anointing. You are miraculous. You are meek.
You are tender. You are patient. You are playful.
You are fierce. You are tangible. You are peace.
You are safe. You are rich. You are just.
You are healing. You are life. You are light.
You are impartation. You are restoration. You are renewal.
You are delightful. You are lovely. You are beautiful.
You are freedom. You are breathtaking. You are strength.
You are breakthrough. You are bread. You are wine.
You are victory. You are splendid. You are pure.
You are resurrection. You are glory. You are radiant.
You are generous. You are intentional. You are gentle.
You are grace. You are mercy. You are Heaven.
You are satisfying. You are inheritance. You are divine.
You are triumphant. You are confidence. You are resolute.
You are limitless. You are inspiration. You are satisfaction
You are wisdom. You are courage. You are infinite.
You are adventure. You are approachable. You are assurance.
You are home. You are deep. You are trustworthy.
You are living. You are comfort. You are close.
You are indescribable. You are creative. You are incomparable.
You are rest. You are enough. You are shelter.
You are laughter. You are oil. You are majestic.

You are vision. You are refreshing. You are irresistible.
You are charming. You are intoxicating. You are relentless.
You are forgiving. You are discernment. You are revelation.
You are salvation. You are destiny. You are breath.
You are glorious. You are everlasting. You are love.
You are everything.

And You are mine.

Song of Songs 5, John 17, Matthew 26, Romans 8, Romans 8:26, Revelation 3, 1 John 2, James 4, Luke 12:15, I John 4:19, Revelation 1, Daniel 10, and Daniel 7, Jeremiah 33, Revelation 3, 1 John 4, Psalms 23, Job 37, Psalm 29, Revelation 19, Isaiah 43, Daniel 3, Psalm 27, Psalm 119

HOLY PILLOW TALK

Deeper Still
Chapter 5, Lukewarm Love

1. Have you noticed the subtle warning signs of a love that is growing lukewarm? As you reflect over the times your love for Jesus has grown cool, what clues or behaviors do you notice leading up to your apathy?

2. On page 100 of this chapter, Jesus prayed to the Father for you. Were His words encouraging? We all have specific things we have been praying for. Ask Jesus to intercede to the Father for you regarding these desires of your heart. Ask Him what He said to the Father. Ask Him what the Father said in return then wait and listen for His responses.

3. Search your life for idols your hands have built, eyes have gazed upon, lips have boasted about, or ears have itched for. Repent aloud for this idolatry.

4. As your intimacy with Jesus grows and matures, there may be those who will not understand your passion. Rejection, mockery, and ridicule from the religious crowd may cross your path. What response does Jesus ask of you? How will you walk with those who do not understand?

5. Go back to pages 108-110, rereading the list of the virtues of Jesus. He truly is all together lovely and complete; ask Him to open your spirit to see and hear Him. Meditate on these attributes and write down what you encounter.

Personal Love Notes to Jesus

Holy Pillow Talk

Personal Love Notes to Jesus

Chapter 6
UNTAMED LOVE

What You Might Experience...

Chapter Six crushes any residual reluctance or inhibitions. This time, *you* will be the one inviting *Him*, rather than Him inviting you. You become the initiator, bringing Jesus incredible delight. Your invitation beckons Him to enter into a higher sphere of intimacy with you, a domain of mutual devotion. As you read, intentionally center your heart and mind on your holy proposal to Him, vulnerably allowing Him to see your hunger on full, unreserved display.

What Others Experienced...

> "The imagery here made me feel excited to connect with Him in a more intimate way. The thought that He wants to be so close to me makes me undone."

> "I greatly enjoyed this chapter. Telling Him how much I love Him through such passion-filled language was freeing to my spirit! I really was born for this!"

> "Something happened within me during this chapter. It was like I knew He felt my love being poured out on Him. I could sense His delight. It was beautiful."

JESUS, MY BRIDEGROOM, SPEAKS TO ME:

I Am overcome with emotion when I see you.

Our union is beautiful. You are more pleasing than any pleasure, more delightful than any delight. You have ravished My heart so deeply that I Am feeble to resist you.

There is no love like yours, My Bride. I Am head over heels in love with you. Even the angelic armies of Heaven stand in awe of your irresistible beauty.

The passion in your eyes melts Me. I can hardly take it; do not look away. I adore your attention and affection. I Am overpowered by your gaze.

Your romantic words of intimate worship rise before Me like the soft waves of the Northern lights. They are full of the colors of our union, expressed as only you can, painting My throne room in passionate, personal shades that leave Me undone. This seamless bond, this zealous loyalty, is what I imagined when I made you, and it leaves Me breathless. Your undying devotion to Me is a fragrant sacrifice.

You have my full attention.

I see how you have savored My truth. You have tasted, chewed, and digested the meat of My Word. You have become balanced, whole, and complete. You have been allowing deep, purifying pruning and purging to take place within you.

I Am deeply pleased. I hang on your every word, for your mouth is full of grace and purity.

Your humility is deeply attractive. You have submitted yourself to Me, considering all other pleasures as emptiness. Abandoning every idol, imposter, and lover has kindled your passion for Me as red hot. Your smile of the true joy you have found in Me has become invincible.

You relented to My pursuing love! Letting go seemed risky, but your desire for Me overcame your reservations. I have been overjoyed to watch you freefall into My secure embrace.

If it still feels foreign to walk free, do not fret. I have got you, My beautiful one! I go before you and behind you. I Am your rearguard. You have chosen to let Me see right into you. Your trust in Me brings Me inexpressible delight! You are My joy!

Many have been called, yet few have been chosen. You, My Bride, chose to endure the process of baptism by fire, allowing Holy Spirit to burn up what does not belong. You arose and came up with Me to the mountain of holiness and consecration. Now you have arisen in My Kingdom for such a time as this. You are My perfect one, the only one for Me. You are unrivaled in beauty, without equal in strength, and beyond compare in devotion.

You are My favorite.

No one has ever seen anything like our love: fresh as the dawn, lovely as the moon, and radiant as the sun.

HOLY PILLOW TALK

His Bride responds:

Our love story is sacred to me.

My heart is on fire and boiling over with passion. You are all I am after! I am focused on You completely, steadfast in my purposeful attention and adoration.

Like an overflowing river, so is my soul bursting to write a love song to You. I am a skillful poet, penning lyrics that are shaped uniquely from who You say I am to You. Your Spirit takes flight in my song, and You capture every syllable. I know You love the music of my life! May it romance You, penetrating Your heart with holy satisfaction.

In joyful reverence, I bow before You, forgetting my past and wholeheartedly severing every attachment to the familiar. Sometimes I close my eyes, trying to remember life before us. Life was hopeless, tasteless, and dark, before You came near. You opened my eyes to see truth, my ears to hear hope and my lips to taste joy.

Thank You.

There is no one like You. You are all I want!

I want You to feel my love.

I do not expect anything in return. Let me lavish You with all I have. Everything I have to offer came from You, and it all belongs to You.

I have one persistent refrain:

I love You!

There is nothing I need besides You. You will always be the only One who makes my heart flutter and burn. The quiver within me testifies to how You make me feel.

I never have to wonder where You are, for Your favorite place is wherever I am. Our garden of delight is our treasured, most intimate place.

Here we feast on one another.

So, come and taste again of all You have planted within me. The fruit of Your love in me is unparalleled in beauty and quality. My life displays and declares the great harvest of Your unending love. The planting, pruning, gathering, pressing, crushing, fermenting, maturing, and testing process has brought forth new wine within me. This rare vintage of new wine is flowing out of my innermost being.

Come and savor the magnificent wine You have fermented within me. The streams of my heart sing of overflowing joy, supernatural miracles, fresh strength, constant peace, and holy authority.

The strategy the enemy designed to destroy me has been turned into something beautiful and powerful because of You, Jesus. Together, we laugh at his foolish plans. I love to hear You laugh. I love watching You throw Your head back and let freedom rumble through Your chest. Your wide smile brings me indescribable elation!

Thank You for victory over my enemies. You never left me in my mess. You came to where I was and rescued me.

Thank You!

Truly I am My Beloved's, and My Beloved is mine. Our romance is wild, spontaneous, and filled with laughter. Our love is made complete here in our constant communion.

I have never been more joyful!

Our sealed covenant makes us one. It is my honor to decrease so that You will increase. What is this wonder, that You desire me more than I desire You, when I stand here consumed for You?

Yet still, increase my capacity ever more toward Your full habitation!

I love that all my inhibitions, hesitations, and reservations have been crushed. Nothing hinders my longing for You. No one but You stands equal to feed the flame in my soul.

I stroll through the orchards and by the stream, looking for signs of spring. I look closely, hoping to see the pink buds bursting into flowers. I lift my voice and sing of Your steadfast love. I watch for You to come and sweep me off my feet. You are constantly on my mind. My longing for You consumes me.

Suddenly, You rapture me away! You knew I was thinking of You. How could You not? We are one! The longing of my heart transports me up and away with You, entirely lifted as though on a chariot of fire!

Once I experienced Your deep places, my desire for You became untamed. You are all I can think about---Your lips, Your touch, Your voice, Your eyes. When You set me free, my worship and love for You became wild and unshackled.

Every time I look at You now, it is as though I am seeing You for the very first time. My burning expectation to encounter You intertwines and sears our hearts together until we are inseparable. Our holy union is exquisite and eternal.

So, it is my honor to lavish my worship on You. I am completely content to stay here kissing Your feet, but You lift me up to sit beside You in heavenly places. I hear You whisper, "Come up here with Me, My Darling."

You return my kiss with Your own, saturating my life and words with supernatural favor and authority. I carry victory in my mouth. You crown me with glory and honor.

I represent You. Nothing can stand against who I am in You.

Thank You for allowing me a seat next to You. Your sacrifice guarantees my victory, now and forever. You are always victorious. Your record is perfect, and now, so is mine. I did not earn Your goodness; You gave it unreservedly.

Goodness is Who You are.

You are more than I could have ever imagined! Your love is simply too much for me to take in. My song pauses for a moment because I cannot find words to match my awe of Your affection for me.

Spontaneous singing and awesome silence swirl between us like a whirlwind of glory. The love songs that rise from this place release greater levels of creativity within me. I purpose to let myself flow in Your river, loosing myself from human measurement. The fetters of failure and fears of foolishness are as ash to me now. I live to worship You! Your opinion of me is the only one that matters.

My melodies invite You to ask me, "My Bride, what do you want? What can I do for you? What do you want from Me?"

My answer, without hesitation, is, "*You! I just want You!*"

I see now I have been thirsty for You for all of my life.

I long to love You more deeply. My heart craves You. Drinking in more of Your glory is my focus. You mean more to me than life itself. Your Presence satisfies me like nothing else. Your strong yet tender embrace is the seat and context of my being.

I am Yours.

What kind of intimate love is this? I am ruined for anything less. I would sing again, but words are entirely insufficient.

I have been marked by Your burning eyes. Just one look was all it took. How can I ever be the same after one glance from You?

One look changed everything.

You were jealous for my attention and now You have it.
You have me. All of me.

How sweet it is to be loved by You! You are my home. Your promises to me never fail. You are my secret place. I stand drenched in Your love and empowered by Your grace.

You know everything there is to know about me. You perceive every movement of my heart and soul, and you understand my thoughts before I do. You are intimately aware of me. You read my heart like an open book, knowing my every word before I utter a syllable.

Yet You lean in to listen to me with fascination.

You know every step I will take before my journey even begins. You have gone into my future to prepare the way, and in kindness, You follow behind me to spare me from the harm of my past.

You are oh, so good to me.

With Your hand of love upon my life, You impart favor and blessings to me. How wonderful, how deep, how incomprehensible! Your understanding brings me wonder, peace and strength.

Where could I go from Your Spirit? Where could I run and hide from Your face? Wherever I go, Your hand guides me and Your strength sustains me. It is impossible to disappear from Your sight.

Your Presence is everywhere. With You, darkness is as light. To You, the night is as bright as the day; there is no difference between the two. Everything You do is marvelously breathtaking. I stand in awe of all You are.

How thoroughly You know me! You formed every part of me when You created me in the secret place, carefully and skillfully shaping me from nothing to something. You brilliantly established my design before my first gene took shape. Before I opened my eyes to the light of my first day, all my days were already recorded in Your book.

Every single moment of every single day, You are thinking of me. How precious and wonderful to consider this: You cherish me constantly in Your every thought! O Lover, Your desires toward me are more than the grains of sand on every shore. Each morning, when I awake from the long night, You are still with me.

Forever, You are with me.

Belonging to You breaks my chest apart in expressions of passion and devotion. The ragged, cheap robes of pride and dignity have been stripped off and burned, and new, expensive robes of humility and elation rest lightly on my shoulders.

Come and watch me, my Love, as I dance for You! My feet were made for the twirling terrain of these mountaintops. You are the source of this joy I feel. I am not ashamed of our love. I do not care who sees me; shame has been completely overwhelmed by confidence! I dance for You extravagantly and without inhibition because my love for You has been untamed!

I live and move in You, with complete abandon.

I am laid bare before You. Consume every part of me as I worship with all my heart, with all my passion, with all the energy of my being!

Every move is with You in mind. You are the Lover of my soul. My every thought and breath are for You.

Jesus, You are so easy to love.

Song of Songs 6, Matthew 22, Revelation 4, Esther 4, Isaiah 52, Psalm 45, Psalm 8, Psalm 73, John 3, Genesis 50, Psalm 59, Psalm 139, Psalms 63, Luke 10, 2 Samuel 6

Deeper Still
Chapter 6, Untamed Love

1. After reading His thoughts for you at the beginning of this chapter, ask Him to allow these words to sink deep into your spirit, soul, and body. Listen for His voice and ask Him to help you live in active belief of these truths.

2. As a prophetic act, purposefully take a moment to laugh at the plan of the enemy. It has failed, falling sterile and noneffective to the ground! Hallelujah! As you laugh, imagine Jesus at your side, laughing with you.

3. To some, "untamed" love may sound flaky, improper, or out of order. This is the shell of religion, poisoning true, vibrant intimacy. Ask Jesus if there are any residual areas of your passion that need to be untamed. Be completely open to His answer to you.

4. Do you sometimes feel confined or restrained in your worship? Ask Him to forgive you for every restraint of pride. As an act of faith, symbolically take off the garments of pride and dignity that have caused you to feel ashamed or conspicuous when offering Jesus your public expressions of affection.

5. Right now, right where you are, take 10 minutes and passionately lavish Him with a spontaneous song of worship and/or words of deep gratitude. Tell Him you have not come for anything in return.

Personal Love Notes to Jesus

Holy Pillow Talk

Personal Love Notes to Jesus

Chapter 7
COVENANT LOVE

What You Might Experience...

Chapter Seven is the crescendo that seals all the prayers and decrees you have embraced through the previous chapters. This intimacy will certainly put your past in perspective, but will also frame the full hope and vision for your future. His words to you are beautifully precise and gentle, pointed and intentional. Slowly and purposefully decree your covenant of love to Him. Trust in His promises to you as you write this new love story together.

What Others Experienced...

"This chapter made me feel a longing to go even deeper with Jesus in our relationship. The boundaries I once had are gone. I feel so free to love and be loved! I have been missing this beautiful part of Him for so long..."

"His tender words calmed and comforted me. I felt a new security and trust with Him. My joy has been refreshed and replenished!"

"This was my favorite chapter for many reasons. It was the perfect culmination of everything I experienced in the previous chapters. All my inhibitions were gone. Our deep intimacy is just beginning! I cannot wait to read through this again!"

HOLY PILLOW TALK

My Bridegroom speaks to Me:

Beloved, I want to describe how I see you—where you were, where you are now, and where you are going. Listen deeply and intently to My thoughts about you.

Ready your heart to listen.

Your feet were once bruised and bleeding from complete bondage. You were shackled, a slave to a list of obligations and burdens. Your voice was weak because your mouth was muzzled.

But look at you now, My Love!

You are bright and shining, without flaw. Your feet are anointed, drenched in oil. You have found your sound, and your sweet voice is becoming strong!

Your beautiful feet wear shoes of peace now. You carry good news, announcing reconciliation, publishing salvation, and proclaiming joy! You are no longer bound to dead works; instead, you move fluidly in expressions of true fruitfulness. Your movement in Me is elegant and graceful because you walk in My ways with dignity and honor.

You are our Father's handiwork, His very best masterpiece!

Out of your innermost being, the fullness of My Spirit is bursting forth with rivers of living water! These waters never fail to satisfy. Your fertile womb births and nurtures an eternal, never-ending harvest. Many sons and daughters are nourished by the holiness and purity you provide.

You have become full of grace and mercy! You are the salt of the earth and the light of the world. There is no hiding the hilltop city you have become, for My light in you shines for everyone to see. Salvation will reach to the ends of the earth as nations are drawn to the blazing brightness of My Presence within you.

Your eyes of revelation are pure, sparkling for all to see. Discernment surrounds you as you fearlessly advance, immune to every subtle detour. Even the best-laid plans of your enemy are as open schemes, and every attempt to harm you falls futile.

My redeeming love crowns you as royalty, for your genealogy is undeniable. You even look like Me. Life, wisdom, and virtue are the center of your thoughts, and as I watch you cling to every good gift from My hand, the delight I find in you is immeasurable.

You stand in complete victory, secure in who you are as My covenant lover. The sight of your surrender is enough to shake heaven and earth.

This is My forever decree, and may it echo across the skies: I will ascend and arise! I take hold of you with My power, possessing every part of you, My fruitful Bride.

I drink in your love, your worship words, as costly wine. I kiss you, and I Am exhilarated with more delight than I have ever known. The kisses of your mouth are intoxicating!

Here I am, Your designer, yet undone all the same.
You have won Me over.

You are valuable, My royal treasure. Indeed, your purpose is to be with Me. You were created for this!

You were created for Me.

HOLY PILLOW TALK

I see all of you, and you see all of Me.

We are one. Our covenant love will never be broken. This bond, our unity, is the most beautiful and all-powerful force that will ever exist.

All of Me, I have given to you.

I Am His Bride:

Jesus, I cherish every word You say to me.

I know Your words are true, and that You mean what You say.

The rain and snow come down from the heavens and remain on the ground to water the earth. They cause the grain to grow, producing seed for the farmer and bread for the hungry.

It is the same with Your Word: potent and effective. When You send it out, it always returns to You with a harvest. It is simply impossible for Your words to fall useless or sterile. Your Word will always accomplish its purpose and will prosper everywhere You send it.

My thoughts are nothing like Your thoughts, and Your ways always supersede my wildest imaginations. The knowledge that Your ways and thoughts are higher than mine—the exact will of all truth and goodness—is reassuring to my soul.

Your words initiated my existence, and they will never fail to sustain me.

When I do not know what to do or which way to go, I trust that You do. I put my faith in You, Lover. There is no limit to Your wisdom and power. I love knowing I am held by You and all Your desires are fulfilled in me.

I am Your heartbeat.

Your eyes never look away from Me. The intensity of Your stare is like a flashing blade of dark and light, overwhelming, suffocating, and all-encompassing. I am all You want, and You are all I want, far more than my every need.

All I do now is for You. Every thought has You at its center. I live for You.

I crave Your touch. I am fascinated by You, and You will never stop pursuing me. Our every moment together reciprocates commitment and passion. I press into You, and You refuse to relent.

I feel like I should split apart under Your gaze, and yet I am forged, galvanized and elevated.

Your Presence places me in the high place of refuge, where I am out of the reach of my enemies.

I am ravished by Your Presence. We speak face to face without barrier, wall, or boundary between us. My face shines, radiating Your glory. You pen love letters to me, filled with hope and wonder. You know me so well, connecting the knowledge in my head with the longings of my heart.

We come away from the noise, nurturing sacred places of connection. I love being alone with You; we sleep in, awakening to the worship songs of the birds. My heart of passion is wide open, and You never tell me to calm down. My fake maturity and feigned serenity are fading away.

I am starting to forget my former restraints.

Because You receive me so fully, I long to display my love for You even more deeply.

I will give all of me to all of You. I know you are pleased as I open myself to receive all You have for me.

Even though some may not comprehend or accept this passionate desire between us, I will not hold back. I will fully express my love for you, no matter who is watching.

You have built within me Your sanctuary, the Holy of Holies, the place where You dwell. I host Your magnificent Presence. As I ponder this reality, I am overwhelmed. Jesus, enter Your resting place within me. May my worship of Your love be a sweet wind in Your lungs.

Deep within my heart are lovesick longings and indescribable groanings for living in constant, covenant union with You. Just one day of unbridled, passionate intimacy with You is better than a thousand days anywhere else.

This is the one thing I ask of You, the only thing I desperately seek:

I must dwell with You all my days.

Making my home in Your beauty is the fulfilment of my life.

Hear me, my Lover! You asked me to seek Your face. My heart responds, pounding with intensity. Lover, Yours is the only face I seek. Your touch is the only touch I crave. You are the single reason for living, so do not withhold Yourself from me for one moment.

Let us drink our fill of one another, without shame or embarrassment. Oneness with You completes me. You alone satisfy.

JESUS, MY BRIDEGROOM, RESPONDS:

Look at you, My Bride!

Clinging to Me, you have risen from the desert wilderness. When I awakened you to My love, your womb came alive with the travail of birthing. You began to ache for more of Me.

You wear My locket of blazing fire around your neck, a covenant seal over your heart. You touch Me with full access. My signet ring fits you with perfection. I have given it to you as a sign of My trust in you, knowing you belong fully to Me. All I have is yours. You wear My authority with humility and wisdom.

I believe in you.

You have been purified, forged, fire-branded, and identified in My white-hot love.

My jealous passion for you is stronger than the chains of death. I Am a holy, devouring, all-consuming fire and My greatest desire is you. I Am surrounding you with My fierce, unrelenting affection and devotion.

Many waters cannot extinguish the flame of our love. A thousand rivers of rejection, pain, trauma, and persecution cannot reduce it. I burn for *you*, My Bride! Even the wide oceans could never smother the raging fire that blazes within you for Me.

I see the hunger and longing in your eyes, and I will fulfill your need. You can have Me. I belong to you.

I will stop at nothing to show you My face.

His Bride speaks:

I am honored to yield to this process of being consumed by You. It no longer feels like sacrifice. I welcome Your impassioned fire. Consume me, wreck me, ravish me, sweet Jesus.

I give to You my every dream, promise, and ambition. I made plans for my future, unaware I had erected idols.

But now I see: my greatest vision is You! Being with You is my destiny! Discovering You is my inheritance! I was created for intimacy with You. I was born for this moment and established for this time. Thank You for rescuing Me from myself.

You are what I have always longed for.

My deepest desire is to know You, and to be fully known by You.

Mark me, Jesus!

Ruin me with Your fierce, uncompromising fire. I want to burn for You and only You. I will meet You at the altar and my life will be the offering. I willingly give You all of me. Take and do whatever pleases You.

Beautiful One, You are my home. I am so deeply in love with You.

You have loved me all the way,
from distracted guest to devoted Bride.

Your faithfulness to me, and My affection for You has transformed me into a stronghold of joy. Now I am a wall of protection and hope for others, modelling the intimacy that will dismantle the enemy's grip on them.

Look what You have done in me! What can I do for You? Ask anything of me; I will say yes.

The twinkle in Your eyes reveals Your favor for me, My Bridegroom-King. Our undefiled romance is a covenant love, devoted and focused. I lean into Your voice, melodious and enchanting. Sing me Your love song again, the one You wrote for me.

I must know everything about You. Will You tell me about Your childhood, Beloved? What is Your favorite song? What brings You the most joy? Share every thought, memory, and preference with me. I have to know You fully.

Hold nothing back from me. Every detail about You is important to me, for my love compels me into rapt attention.

You take great delight in me and rejoice over me with singing. I love listening to the songs You have written for me. Serenade me again, whispering Your psalms in my ear while we slow dance together.

Eagerly, I put my hand in Yours. You pull me close, thankful for my enthusiasm in asking You to dance. You grin with glee to be pursued, telling me how much You love that I am initiating deeper intimacy. Slowly, rhythmically, romantically we dance, cheek to cheek.

I am caught in Your caress. I breathe of You, as though I have never breathed until now.

In this moment, I am more alive than I ever have been.

I have seen enough to believe: I am Your dream, Your portal and ambassador in the earth. I am Your voice, Your compassionate, manifested hands and feet.

Your appetite is filled with an insatiable hunger for me.

Jesus, please pull me closer. You answer this invitation with delight and expectancy! We lock eyes and I lose myself in You. I will not look away ever again, because You have taught me who I am.

I rest my head on Your chest. I am overjoyed to hear my heart synchronize with Yours. Our pulsating hearts now flow with the same rhythmic cadence.

The smell of Your skin intensifies my desperation to be close to You. This is all that matters. This is what I live for: communion with You.

This is my most favorite place.

I whisper in Your ear, my need for more of You. You smile slowly and Your arms tighten around me. Your answer is low, meant only for me: "Of course."

You pour Your love out upon me, and I weep to be so loved.

This holy place is where You share with me what is on Your heart. You tell me Your secrets. There are no boundaries between us.

Our covenant love can never be broken.

We will forever be as One.

I love our Holy Pillow Talk.

Song of Songs 7 & 8, Isaiah 52, Ephesians 6, John 7, Matthew 5, Isaiah 49, Isaiah 55, Psalms 84, Psalms 27, Hebrew 12, Zephaniah 3, John 13

Deeper Still
Chapter 7, Covenant Love

1. Sometimes, our focus falls out of order. Our first love and all our devotion belong to Jesus, overflowing into our family and throughout our life's work and activities. If your attention has been out of alignment, especially if you serve in any aspect of ministry, ask Him to forgive you, and to properly restructure your attention.

2. Have you ever worried that you may have missed your destiny or purpose? When we establish intimacy with Jesus as our first love, we will always be fulfilled. It is never too late to renew Your intimacy with Him. Ask Him to renew your mind, reinvigorating your heart-to-heart and eye-to-eye communion.

3. Have you ever asked Jesus something personal about Himself? List three personal questions you would like to ask Him. Now, ask Him! Intentionally listen for His answers throughout the upcoming days and weeks.

4. Cue up an intimate worship song. Stand up and ask Jesus to slow dance with you. If you feel uneasy or awkward, try to push through! Make this a weekly practice and remember to journal your experiences with Him. What does He feel like, sound like, smell like, look like?

5. As you turn out the lights tonight, picture your head resting upon Jesus as you are falling asleep. Imagine gazing into His eyes of love. Tell Him how He makes you feel and ask Him what is on His heart. Listen as He, Your Bridegroom, shares His secrets with you.

PERSONAL LOVE NOTES TO JESUS

Personal Love Notes to Jesus

About The Author

Amanda Hill is the co-founder of Kingdom River International, a non-profit ministry to the nations, and founder of Amanda Hill Ministries. She is a licensed, ordained, and commissioned minister of the gospel. An apostolic prophet and gifted teacher, Amanda is a rare blend of fire and water. Her unique prophetic insight, refreshing transparency, and humorous delivery enables authentic encounters with Jesus that engage, encourage, and equip believers.

First and foremost, Amanda is a lover of Jesus, devoted to David (her husband of nearly 23 years) and their amazing children Mason, Eliana, and Raegan Elizabeth (who is in the presence of Jesus). The Hill family are proud to be born and raised Charlestonians, believing nothing could be finer than to live in South Carolina, y'all.

To Contact Amanda

www.amandahill.org | www.kingdomriver.org

Made in United States
Troutdale, OR
11/04/2024